Emerald Law

The English Legal System

Anthony Chadwick

Emerald Publishing

British Cataloguing in Publication data. A catalogue record is available for this book from the British Library.

ISBN
978-1-84716-556-5

Printed in the United Kingdom by 4edge www.4edge.co.uk

Cover Design by Bookworks Islington

Contents

Introduction

1. The Framework of Law   13
International law   13
National law   13
Public law   13
Constitutional law   14
Administrative law   14
Criminal law   14
Private law   14
Distinctions between civil and criminal cases   14
Defining law   16
Law and morality   17
Law and justice   17
Rights and duties   18

2. The Development of Law   19
Customs   19
General customs   19
Local customs   19
Common law   20
Equity   21
Judicial precedents   22
Ratio decidendi   22
Obiter dicta   23
Original precedent   23
Binding precedent   24
Persuasive precedent   24
The hierarchy of courts and precedent   24
The European Court of Justice   25
The Supreme Court   26

The Court of Appeal   26
Divisional Courts   26
Courts of First Instance   27
The High Court   27
Inferior Courts   27
Use of Practice Statement   29
Distinguishing, overruling and
reversing previous decisions   30
Advantages and disadvantages of precedent   30
Disadvantages of precedent   31
Reporting cases   32

3. Parliament and Acts of Parliament   **33**

Parliament   33
Judges in the Supreme Court   33
Factors influencing law making at a government level   34
The pre-legislative process   34
Introducing an Act of Parliament   34
The distinction between public and private bills   35
The Parliamentary process   36
Commencement of an Act   39
Parliamentary sovereignty   39

4. European Law   **41**

Recent history   41
The Council of Ministers   41
The Commission   43
The Assembly   43
The European Court of Justice   44
Discretionary referrals   46
The Court of First Instance   46

Regulations 47
Directives 47
Conflict between European law and national law 49

5. Statutory interpretation of law 51

Liberal approach v Purposive approach 51
The literal rule 52
The golden Rule 52
The mischief rule 52
Rules of language 53
The *ejusdem generis* rule 53
Presumptions 55
Unified approach to interpretation 55
The purposive approach 56

6 The legal profession 57

Solicitors 67
Complaints against solicitors 58
Office for the Supervision of solicitors 58
Barristers 58
Queens Counsel 60
Complaints against barristers 60
The judiciary 61
Types of judge 62
Superior judges 62
Inferior judges 62
Lords Justices of Appeal 63
High Court judges 63
Circuit judges 63
Recorders 63
District judges 64

Law officers 64
The Attorney General 64
The Solicitor general 65
The Director of Public Prosecutions 65
Magistrates 66
Duties of magistrates 66

7 Civil Cases **71**

Commencing a case in the county court 71
Which court? 72
Issuing a claim against another party 73
Defending a claim 73
Small claims 74
Fast-track cases 74
Multi-track cases 75
The High Court 75
The Single Family Court 75
The Queens Bench Division 77
Commercial court 77
Admiralty court 77
The Chancery Division 77
Family Divisions 78
The Civil Procedure Rules 78
Appellate courts 79
Divisional Courts 79
Queens bench Divisional Court 79
Chancery Divisional Court 79
Court of Appeal (Civil Division) 80
The Supreme Court 80
Appeal routes in civil cases 81
Appeals from the county court 81
Appeals from small claims 81

Appeals from the High Court   81
Further appeals   81
Remedies in civil cases   82
Special damages   82
General damages   82
Nominal damages   82
Exemplary damages   82
Equitable remedies   83
Specific performance   83
Rescission   83
Rectification   84
Alternative Dispute resolution   84

8 Criminal cases-Police Powers   **85**

Police powers   86
Powers to arrest-serious arrestable offences   86
Powers to stop and search   87
Voluntary searches   87
Other powers to stop and search   87
Roadside checks   88
The power to search premises   88
Power to enter premises without warrant   89
To prevent breach of the peace   89
Searching premises with consent of occupier   89
Unlawful entry and search   89
Powers of arrest   90
Arrestable offences   90
PACE Section 24-arrests by police and private
Citizens   90
PACE Section 25   91
Other rights of arrest   91
Breach of the peace   92

Right to search 92
Powers to detain suspect 92
Rights of detained people 93
Police interviews 93
Right to silence 94
Searches, fingerprints and samples 94
Complaints against police 95
The Independent Police Complaints Commission 95

9 Hearing Criminal Cases 96

Pre-trial hearings 96
Categories of criminal offence 96
Bail 97
Bail sureties 98
The Crown Prosecution Service 99
Criminal courts 100
The role of the Magistrates Court 100
Summary trials 101
Triable either way cases 102
Sending cases to the Crown Court 103
Committal proceedings 103
Role of the court clerk 103
Youth Courts 103
Appeals from the Magistrates Court 104
Further appeals from the House of Lords 104
The Crown Court 104
Preliminary matters 105
The Indictment 105
Disclosure 105
The trial 106
Appeals 107
Sentencing 109

Custodial sentences   110
Community sentences   110
Fines   111
Discharges   111
Other powers available to the courts   112
Young offenders   112
Attendance centre orders   112
Supervision orders   113
Fines for young offenders   113
Reparation orders   113
Discharges   114
Reprimands and warnings   114
Responsibility of parents   114
Parenting orders   115
Offenders who are mentally ill   115
Anti-Social Behaviour Orders   116

10 Juries   **117**

Civil cases   117
Selecting a jury   118
Criminal cases   120
Majority verdicts   120

11 Legal aid and advice   **121**

The Legal Aid Agency   121
Governance   121
Legal aid and financial help   122
The different types of civil legal aid   123
Who can provide legal aid services ?   123
Financial conditions for getting civil legal aid   128
Repaying solicitors costs at the end of a case   129

Civil Legal Advice Helpline   129
Legal Aid for criminal cases   130
Free legal help   131
Paying court fees if getting legal aid   133
Other sources of free legal help   133
Conditional fee agreements   133

Index

Introduction

This second edition of Emerald Law-Guide to the English Legal System is wide ranging and covers all the main areas of our complex legal system in depth.

For the average person, the legal system in this country can appear mystifying. All they know is that the process of funding legal cases costs a lot of money. However, for most of us in our lives, one way or another, we will find ourselves in court. The need for good advice will be paramount.

It is very important for a citizen to have a clear idea of how the legal system operates and who is who in the system, the role of the judiciary, the European Courts and also the availability of funding if a case needs to go to court and is proving to expensive.

One of the main axioms of the last ten years or so has been access to justice. How easily can individuals and others access the legal system in this country. With the advent of the coalition government it seems that legal aid will be restricted making it harder for people to access legal advice.

This introduction to the English Legal System should prove invaluable to all, student, professional and layperson.

Anthony Chadwick 2015

1

The Framework of Law

Law covers a wide variety of areas. There are different categories of law: national law; international law which is divided into public and private law and further sub-categories discussed later.

International law

International law concerns Itself with inter-nation disputes and conflict. This law, in the main, derives from various treaties which have been agreed over time between different governments.

National law

This is the law which applies within each individual nation. Within national law there is a distinction between public and private law. Public law involves the government or state in some way and private law is concerned with disputes and conflict between individuals and businesses. Public and private law, as mentioned can be further sub-divided.

Public law

There are three distinct areas of public law:

1. Constitutional law

Constitutional law controls and sets out the framework for government, and methods of government.

2. Administrative law

This controls how the ministers of government, both national and local, can operate. A key part of administrative law is that of the right to judicial review of decisions made by government.

3. Criminal law

Criminal law deals with the types of behaviour, whether individual or on a business level, which are considered outside the boundaries of the general law and accepted moral codes and which are punishable. A person who commits a crime is said to have offended against the State and the State has the right to prosecute them and punish them if found guilty.

Private law

Private law is usually termed civil law and there are many differing branches. The main ones dealing with everyday matters are family law, contract law, tort (negligence) company law and employment law. Civil law is very different in nature from criminal law. Whereas criminal law deals with crimes against the state private or civil law deals with disputes between individuals

Distinctions between criminal law cases and civil cases

There are key differences between criminal and civil cases. The cases take place in different courts. In general, criminal law cases will be heard in either Magistrates Courts or the Crown Court. Civil cases are heard either in the High Court or, more often than not, in the County Court. Some civil cases, especially matters concerning family, can be heard in the Magistrates Court.

In criminal cases, the terminology used to describe key personnel is different to that of those involved in civil cases. The person commencing a criminal case is called a prosecutor, whilst in civil cases they are called the claimant.

In criminal cases, the terminology used generally is different. A person is either found guilty or not guilty. In a civil case a defendant is found liable or not liable. At the end of a criminal case, the person, if found guilty, will be punished and sentenced appropriately. In a civil case, the person if found to be liable will be ordered to put right the matter. This is usually done by an award of money as compensation, known as damages although other remedies may be ordered.

In criminal cases, the standard of proof is very high. A criminal case must be proven beyond all reasonable doubt. Civil cases are proved on the balance of probabilities. This is a lower standard of proof.

Overleaf is a summary of civil and criminal law cases.

	Civil cases	Criminal cases
Object of law	To uphold the rights of individuals	To maintain law and order
Person starting case	Individuals who are affected	Usually State through police or Crown Prosecution Service
Terminology	Claimant	Prosecutor
Courts	County Court or High Court or Tribunal	Magistrates court or Crown Court
Standard of proof	The balance of probability	Beyond reasonable doubt
People making Decision	Judge	Magistrates or jury
Decision	Liable or not liable	Guilty or not guilty
Powers of court	Usually damages, injunction, performance of contract rescission or rectification	Prison, fine, community order, discharge etc.

Defining law

Having considered the various divisions of law it is now time to consider definitions of law. One broad definition of law was that provided by Sir John Salmond. He defined the law as being 'the body of principles recognised and applied by the state in the administration of justice'. This neatly encapsulates the meaning and application of law in one brief sentence.

Law applies throughout a country to people generally. There are other sets of rules applied more individually to people and organisations, for example rules governing sports or rules which have developed as a result of local customs and traditions.

Law and morality

Moral values of communities set out a framework for how people should behave. Concepts of morality differ from culture to culture, although there are common denominators, for example outlawing extreme and harmful behaviour such as rape or murder. Morality often springs from a religious base, the bible for Christians and the Koran for Muslims are key examples. The law of a country will, usually, reflect the moral values accepted by most of a country but will differ in certain aspects. One example is that adultery is often considered a crime in Muslim countries but not so in Christian countries.

In England and Wales there has been a move away from religious belief and the development of law reflects this. For example a limited form of euthanasia has been accepted as legal, as reflected in the ruling in Airedale NHS Trust v Bland (1993), where it was ruled that medical staff could withdraw life support systems from a patient who could breathe unaided but who was in a persistent vegetative state. Similarly, with abortion which is legalised. Whilst there are many groups who believe that euthanasia and abortion are immoral the law has moved differently.

Law and justice

Although justice is the main goal of the law it doesn't always provide a just outcome. There is the problem of defining justice as was outlined by Lord Wright, who said:

' the guiding principle of a judge in deciding cases is to do justice; that is justice according to the law, but still justice. I have not found any satisfactory definition of justice…what is just in a particular case is what appears just to the just man, in the same way as what is reasonable appears to be reasonable to the reasonable man'.

In many circumstances people's concepts of justice will be different. For example, the situation where a person uses force to repel a burglar and injures that person. This has been the cause of many a heated debate, from one end of the spectrum where it is thought right to be able to defend and kill in the process to the other end where it is seen as only right to defend but not injure. No doubt this debate will rage on forever more. This example highlights differing views on concepts of justice.

Rights and duties of individuals under the law

The law gives rights to individuals. It also gives methods of enforcing those rights if violated. The law also imposes duties on individuals. Rights and duties run through many areas such as contract and employment and also runs through criminal law, imposing a duty on the individual to obey the law and a right of the state to punish.

****

2

The Development of Law

The law in England and Wales has developed gradually over time. Law has been developed in a number of different ways, and the methods of developing law are known as sources of law. Historically, the most important ways were custom and decisions of judges. Parliament became more powerful in the eighteenth and nineteenth centuries, with Acts of Parliament becoming the main source of new laws, although judicial decisions were, and are, still important. During the twentieth century, statute law and judicial decisions continued to be the main sources of law, but increasingly two new sources of law became important: delegated legislation and European legislation. Together, all these sources of law have combined to create the present day legal system.

Customs

Customs are rules of behaviour which develop in a community. There are two main types of custom: general and local customs.

General customs

General customs are common customs which have developed and have been absorbed over time into law.

Local customs

Local customs is a term used where a person claims that he or she is entitled to some local right, such as a right of way or the right to use land in a certain way, because this is what has happened locally over time. Judge have a test of what constitutes local customs. These are as follows:

- The custom must have existed since 'time immemorial
- The custom must have been exercised peaceably openly and as of right
- The custom must be definite as to locality, nature and scope
- The custom must be reasonable

It is very rare for a new custom to be considered by courts nowadays. There have been certain exceptions. For example, in Egerton v Harding (1974) the court decided that there was a customary duty to fence land against cattle straying from the common. Although customs develop they are not part of the law until recognised by the courts.

Common law

The legal system historically could not rely on customs alone. In Anglo-Saxon times there were local courts that decided disputes but it was not until after the Norman conquest in 1066 that a more organised system of courts developed. Norman kings realised that control of the country was that much easier if the legal system was also controlled. William the Conqueror set up the Curia Regis (The Kings Court) and appointed judges to hear disputes from the nobles. In addition to this central court, judges were sent to major towns to decide important cases.

In the time of Henry 11 (1154-89) these tours became more regular and the country was divided up into circuits, or areas for the judges to visit. Initially the judges would use the local customs or the old Anglo-Saxon laws to decide cases. On return to London the judges would discuss customs and gradually these evolved into a uniform or common law.

Common law is the basis of our law today, an unwritten law that developed from customs and judicial decisions. The phrase 'common law' is still used to distinguish laws that have been developed by judicial decisions, from laws that have been created by statute or other legislation. For example murder is a common law crime whilst theft is a statutory crime.

Common law also has another meaning. It is used to distinguish between rules that were developed by the common law courts (the Kings Courts) and the rules of equity which were developed by the Lord Chancellor and the Chancery Courts.

Equity

Historically this is an important source still playing a part today with many of our legal concepts having developed from equitable principles. The word 'equity' has a meaning of fairness and this is the basis on which it operates.

Equity developed because of problems in the common law. Only certain types of cases were recognised. The law was also very technical; if there was an error in the formalities the person making the claim would lose the case. People who could not obtain justice in the common law courts appealed to the King. Most of these cases were referred to the Kings Chancellor. This was because the Chancellor based his decisions on principles of natural justice and fairness, making a decision on what seemed right in a particular case as opposed to the strict following of previous precedents. Account was also taken of what the parties had originally intended.

To ensure that decisions were fair, new procedures were introduced such as subpoenas, which ordered a witness to attend court. New remedies for compensation were developed which were able to compensate plaintiffs more fully than those previously used. The main equitable remedies were: injunctions; specific performance; rescission and rectification. These are all still in use today and will be explained more fully later on in this book.

Judicial precedents

The doctrine of precedents

Judicial precedent refers to the source of law where decisions of judges in the past create law for future judges to follow. This source of law is also known as case law and is a major source of law.

The English system of precedent is based on the Latin maxim *stare decisis et non quieta movere* which is usually shortened to *stare decisis* and which translated means 'stand by what has been decided and do not unsettle the established'. This supports the idea of fairness and certainty in law.

Ratio Decidendi

Precedent is only relevant and can only be effective if the reasons for past decisions are known. Judges will outline reasons for decisions and the rationale for a judgement outlining the principles of law used. These principles are an important part of any judgement and are known as the *ratio decidendi* which means the reason for deciding. This is what creates the precedent for future judges to follow.

Obiter Dicta

The remainder of the judgement is called *obiter dicta* (other things said) and judges in future cases do not have to follow it.

Original precedent

If the point of law in a case has never been decided before, then whatever the judge decides will form a new precedent for future cases to follow. As there are no past cases for a judge to base his decision on, he is likely to look at cases which are the closest in principle and he may decide to use similar rules. This way of arriving at a judgement is called reasoning by analogy. The idea of creating new law by analogy can be seen in Hunter and others v Canary Wharf Limited and London Docklands Development Corporation (1995). Part of the decision involved whether the interference with television reception was capable of constituting an actionable private nuisance. The facts of the case were that the main tower Canary Wharf built in the Isle of Dogs East London, was 250 metres high and 50 metres square. The claimant and others claimed damages from the defendant for continuing interference over a number of years with the television reception in the area as a result of the height of the tower.

In the Court of Appeal, the Lord Justice Pill stated:

'Lord Irving (counsel for the defendants) submits that interference with television reception by reason of the presence of a building is properly to be regarded as analogous to loss of aspect (view). To obstruct the receipt of television signals by the erection of a building between the point of receipt and the source is not in law a nuisance............... I accept the importance of television in the lives of people. However, in my judgement the erection or presence *of a building in the line of sight between a television transmitter and other properties is not actionable as an interference with the use and enjoyment of land. The analogy with loss of prospect is compelling. The loss of a view, which may be of the greatest importance to householders, is not actionable and neither is the mere presence of a building in the site lines to the television transmitter'.*

Binding precedent

This is a precedent from an earlier case which must be followed even if the judge in the later case does not agree with the principle. A binding precedent is only created where the facts of the second case are sufficiently similar to the original case.

Persuasive precedent

This is a precedent that is not binding on the court but the judge may consider it and decide that it is a correct principle and is persuaded that it should be followed.

Persuasive precedent comes from a number of sources:

- Courts lower in the hierarchy
- Decisions by the Judicial Committee of the Privy Council
- Statements made obiter dicta
- A dissenting judgement
- Decisions of courts in foreign countries.

The hierarchy of courts and precedent

In England and Wales courts operate a rigid hierarchy of judicial precedents. Every court is bound to follow any decision made by a court above it in the hierarchy.

In general appellate courts (appeal courts) are bound by their own decisions.

The diagram below indicates the hierarchy of courts in the UK.

THE STRUCTURE OF THE COURTS

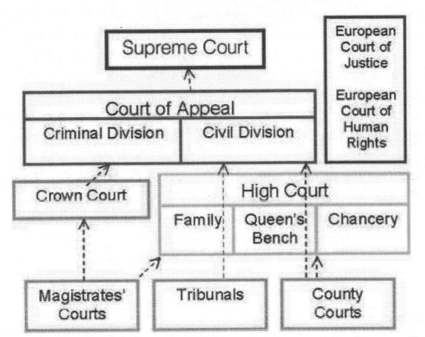

The European Court of Justice

The highest court affecting the legal system in England and Wales is the European Court of Justice. This has been the case since 1973. For points of European law, a decision made by this court is binding on all other courts in England and Wales. There are still laws unaffected by European Union law and for these the House of Lords is the supreme court.

Supreme Court

The Supreme Court of the United Kingdom

The Supreme Court of the United Kingdom was established by the Constitutional Reform Act of 2005. The Court started work on October 1st 2009. It has taken over the judicial functions of the House of Lords, which were exercised by the Lords of Appeal in Ordinary Law (Law Lords), the 12 professional judges appointed as members of the House of Lords to carry out its judicial business. It will also assume some functions of the Judicial Committee of the Privy Council.

The court is the Supreme Court (court of last resort, highest appellate court) in all matters under English law, Welsh law (to the extent that the National Assembly for Wales makes laws for Wales that differ from those in England) and Northern Irish law. It will not have authority over criminal cases in Scotland, where the High Court of Justiciary will remain the supreme criminal court. However, it will hear appeals from the civil court of session, just as the House of Lords did before.

Court of appeal

The court of appeal is next in the hierarchy and has two divisions, civil and criminal. Both of these divisions are bound to follow the decisions of the European Court of Justice and the Supreme Court. They must also follow past decisions of their own although there are exceptions to the rule and the Court of Appeal (Criminal Division) is more flexible where it involves the liberty of the subject.

Divisional courts

The three divisional courts, Queens bench, Chancery and Family are bound by decisions of the European Court of Justice, the

Supreme Court and the Court of Appeal. The divisional courts are also bound by their own past decisions, although there are some exceptions.

Courts of first instance

This term means any court where the original trial of a case is held. Appeal courts do not hear any original trials only appeals from those trials. Courts of first instance rarely ever create precedents only following decisions of courts above them.

The High Court

The High Court is bound by decisions of all courts above it and in turn it binds the lower courts.

Inferior courts

Inferior courts are the Crown Court, the County Court and the Magistrates Court. They are bound to follow decisions of all higher courts. It is very unlikely that a decision by a lower court can create a precedent. The one exception is that a ruling on a point of law by a judge in a Crown Court will bind the Magistrates Court.

The Tribunal System

Tribunals form part of the civil justice system in the UK, alongside ordinary courts. Parliament makes decisions about the structure of the court and tribunal system which change over time. Currently, a reform of the tribunal system is underway. Under the previous system, which still exists to a large extent, there are many different types of tribunal, each focusing on a specific area of law. There are 20 or so tribunals that sit regularly, and many more than sit less frequently. The Tribunals Service is the organisation created to administer the tribunals. Together, more than 130 tribunals deal with approximately one million cases per year, which is more than any other part of the justice system. The geographical jurisdiction of tribunals varies, with some extending beyond England and Wales to include Scotland and/or Northern Ireland as well.

The main tribunals are:

- Employment tribunals

- Immigration Services Tribunal

- Lands Tribunal

- Social Security & Child Support Commissioners

- The Criminal Injuries and Compensation Appeals Panel

- The Mental Health Review Tribunal

- Pensions Appeal Tribunals

- Asylum & Immigration Tribunal

The Tribunals, Courts and Enforcement Act 2007 brought about changes to the tribunal structure. It set up a two-tiered system, the First–tier Tribunal is a new generic tribunal whose main function is to hear appeals against decisions of the Government when the tribunal has been given jurisdiction. Most tribunals are being combined into the First–tier Tribunal.

The Upper Tribunal has been created to deal with appeals from, and enforcement of, decisions of the First-tier Tribunal. It is a court of record with jurisdiction throughout the United Kingdom. Its main functions are:

- To hear appeals from the decisions of local tribunals

- To hear and decide certain cases that do not go through the First-tier Tribunal

- To exercise powers of judicial review in certain circumstances

- To deal with enforcement of decisions, directions and orders made by tribunals

Use of Practice Statement

Until 1966, the House of Lords in the United Kingdom was bound to follow all of its previous decisions under the principle of stare decisis, even if this created "injustice" and "unduly restrict(s) the proper development of the law" (London Tramways Co. v London City Council [1898] AC 375). The Practice Statement 1966 is authority for the House of Lords (now Supreme Court) to depart from their previous decisions.

Text of the Practice Statement:

Their Lordships regard the use of precedent as an indispensable foundation upon which to decide what is the law and its application to individual cases. It provides at least some degree of certainty upon which individuals can rely in the conduct of their affairs, as well as a basis for orderly development of legal rules. Their Lordships nevertheless recognise that too rigid adherence to precedent may lead to injustice in a particular case and also unduly restrict the proper development of the law. They propose therefore, to modify their present practice and, while treating formal decisions of this house as normally binding, to depart from a previous decision when it appears to be right to do so. In this connection they will bear in mind the danger of disturbing retrospectively the basis on which contracts, settlement of property, and fiscal arrangements have been entered into and also the especial need for certainty as to the criminal law. This announcement is not intended to affect the use of precedent elsewhere than in this House. — Lord Gardiner's statement in the House of Lords, July 26, 1966.

Distinguishing, overruling and reversing previous decisions

Distinguishing is a method used by a judge to avoid following a past decision which otherwise would have to be followed. It means that the judge finds that the material facts of the case he is following are sufficiently different for him to draw a distinction between the present case and the previous case. He is not then bound by the previous case. Overruling is where a court in a later case decides that the legal rule in a previous case is wrong. Overruling may occur when a higher court overrules a decision by a lower court, for example the Supreme Court overruling a decision by the Court of Appeal. Reversing is where a court higher up in the hierarchy overturns the decision of a lower court on appeal in the same case.

Advantages and disadvantages of precedent in the law

There are advantages and disadvantages to the way judicial precedent operates in England and Wales.

Advantages

The main advantages to the operation of precedent are:

Certainty
Because the courts follow past decisions, people know what the law is and how it is likely to be applied in their case. Lawyers advise clients on the likely outcome of cases and it also allows people to

operate their businesses in the certainty that what they do is within the law.

Consistency and fairness

It is seen as just and fair that similar cases are decided in the same way.

Precision

As the principles of law are set out in actual cases, the law becomes very precise.

Flexibility

There is room for the law to change as the Supreme Court can use the Practice Statement to overrule cases.

Time- saving

Precedent can be considered a useful time saving device as where a principle has been established, cases with similar facts are unlikely to go through the lengthy process of litigation.

Disadvantages

Rigidity

The fact that lower courts have to follow decisions of higher courts, together with the fact that the Court of Appeal has to follow its own past decisions, can make the law too inflexible so that bad decisions made in the past can be perpetuated.

Complexity

There are many reported cases and it may be complex and time consuming to find the right case on which to base a decision.

Illogical distinctions

The use of distinguishing to avoid past decisions can lead to illogical distinctions so that some areas of law have become very complex.

Reporting cases

Written law reports have existed in England and Wales since the 13th century. Reports right from the early times were inaccurate and difficult to follow. In 1865 the Incorporated Council of Law was set up, controlled by the courts. Law reports became more accurate and precise, with judgements being noted word for word. This accuracy of reports was one of the factors in the development of the strict doctrine of precedent. There are also other well established reports today, notably the All England Series (abbreviated to All ER) and the weekly law Reports (WLR). The internet also provides reports, websites such as www. lawreports.co.uk and www.publications.parliament.uk.

****

3

Parliament and Acts of Parliament

The main legislative body in the United Kingdom is Parliament. Laws passed by Parliament are known as Acts of Parliament, or statutes. This source of law is usually referred to as statute law. In addition to Parliament, power is delegated to government ministers and their departments to make detailed rules and regulations which supplement Parliament. These regulations are delegated legislation and are called statutory instruments.

Parliament consists of the House of Commons and the House of Lords. Both houses must be in favour of a bill, vote in its favour, before it can become law.

The people who sit in the House of Commons are elected Members of Parliament, representing their constituencies who elected them.

The House of Lords is somewhat different consisting of hereditary peers, life peers, judges who are law lords and the most senior bishops in the Church of England. The Lords has, in the past few years, undergone radical reform with the process still continuing. Essentially, the process whereby hereditary peers dominated the Lords has ended with a more democratic approach being sought.

Judges in the Supreme Court

As discussed, the Supreme Court is the most senior court in England and Wales. Only the 12 Law Lords are allowed to sit in this court

Factors influencing law making at a government level

When they are formed, Governments have programmes of reforms. These are set out in government manifestos at election time and reinforced during the Queens speech at the opening of Parliament. Basically, most new legislation emanates from government policy.

There are other influences at play which affect what laws are enacted. One such major influence is European legislation. New Acts are passed to bring our law in line with European legislation. Other outside influences include proposals for law reform put forward by law reform agencies, commissions or enquiries into the effectiveness of existing law. Specific events can also lead to changes in the law, events such as the massacre of young children at a school in Dunblane in 1996 which resulted in Firearms Legislation in 1997. Another outside influence is that of pressure groups who cause government to reconsider law in specific areas. One such instance was in 1994 when the government reduced the age of homosexual consent from 21 to 18. In 2000, this was further reduced to 16.

The pre-legislative process

On major matters a minister with responsibility for a specific area will issue a Green paper. This is a consultative document on a topic with the government's views on law reform. Following receipt of the views of all interested parties a White Paper will then be issued with its firm proposals for new law.

Introducing an Act of Parliament

The majority of Acts of Parliament are introduced by the government of the day. They are initially drafted by civil service lawyers known as Parliamentary Counsel to the Treasury.

When the proposed Act has been drafted it is published as a Bill. It will only progress to become an Act of Parliament if it completes all the stages successfully in Parliament. The drafting of Bills is painstaking and exact and must be framed in terms which are unambiguous. This is against a backdrop of the inevitable pressure of time.

Bills can also be sponsored by individual MP's. The Parliamentary process allows for a ballot in each session in which 20 private members are selected who can then take their turn in presenting a Bill to Parliament. Time for debate of these Bills is limited, usually being debated on a Friday and only a few members have a realistic chance of introducing a Bill on their chosen topic. Only a few Private Members Bills become law. Notable Acts passed have been the Abortion Act of 1967 which legalised abortion and the Marriage Act 1994 which allowed marriage in any registered place.

Backbenchers can also try to introduce a Bill through what is known as the 'Ten Minute Rule' under which any MP can make a speech of up to 10 minutes supporting the introduction of new legislation.

Members of the House of Lords can also introduce Private Members Bills.

The distinction between public and private Bills

A public Bill involves matters of public policy which will affect the country at large or a significant section of the country. Most Government Bills are in this category. However, some Bills are passed aimed at individuals or company's which are private Bills.

The Parliamentary process

In order for a Bill to become an Act of Parliament, it will usually have to be passed by both House of Commons and House of Lords. In each House there is a long process. A bill may commence in either House with the exception of finance Bills which must commence in the Commons. There are a number of stages which all Bills must go through to become law:

1. First reading

This is a formal procedure where the name and aims of the Bill are read out. There will be a vote on whether the House wants to consider the Bill further. The vote can be verbal, where the speaker of the House asks the members as a whole how they vote and they shout out 'Aye' or 'No'. If it is clear that all members are in agreement, either for or against then there is no need for a formal vote. If it is not clear then a formal vote will be taken. Members of the House will leave the Chamber and then re-enter by one of two doors signifying for or against. Tellers total the votes for and against and declare the result to the Speaker.

2. Second reading

The second reading is the main debate on the whole Bill in which MP's debate the principles underlying the Bill. No one may speak without being called on to do so by the Speaker. At the end of the process a vote is taken in the same way as the first reading. To proceed to the next stage the Bill must be voted in favour of.

3. Committee stage

This stage is where a detailed examination of the Bill is undertaken by a committee of between 16 and 50 MP's. This is called a Standing Committee which is a committee chosen specifically to examine the Bill. This committee is made up by opposition and minority parties as well as the Government who will have a majority. Membership is made up in direct proportion to parties seats in the Houses of Parliament and will consist of people with a knowledge of the matter in hand.

4. Report stage

At the Committee stage amendments to various clauses in the Bill may have been voted on and passed. The report stage is where the Committee reports back to the House on the amendments.

5. Third reading

This stage is the final vote on the Bill. Having reached this stage it is unlikely to fail.

6. The House of Lords

If the Bill emanated from the Commons it will now go to the Lords where it will go through the same five stages and if amendments are made by the Lords to the Bill then it will go back to the Commons to consider those amendments. If the Bill emanated from the Lords then it will go to the Commons.

7. Royal assent

The final stage is where the monarch gives approval to the Bill and it then becomes an Act of Parliament. This is a formality. Under the Royal Assent Act 1961, the Monarch will not even have the text of

Bills to which she is assenting. She will only have the title of the Bill. The diagram below summarises the process of legislation from drafting of a Bill to Act of Parliament through the House of Commons.

The Bill is Drafted

|

First reading in the House of Commons

|

Second reading in the House of Commons

|

Committee stage

|

Report stage

|

Third reading in the House of Commons

|

Same procedures in The House of Lords

|

Royal assent

The power of the House of Lords to reject a Bill is limited by the Parliament Acts of 1911 and 1949. These Acts allow a Bill to become law even if the Lords reject it provided that the Bill is re-introduced into the House of Commons in the next session of Parliament and goes through all the stages once again. The principle behind the Acts is that the House of Lords is not an elected body and its function is not to oppose the will of the elected House of Commons but to refine the law.

Commencement of an Act

Following Royal Assent the Act becomes law on midnight of that day, unless another date has been set for it to become law. This has become the norm, where a date is set where it should become law. A commencement order will be issued by the appropriate minister. In many cases, sections of an Act come into force at different times which causes confusion. This again is becoming something of a norm. One such Act was the Criminal Justice Act of 2003.

Parliamentary sovereignty

Parliamentary law is sovereign over other forms of law in England and Wales. This means that an Act of Parliament can completely supersede any custom, judicial precedent, delegated legislation or previous Act of Parliament. However, European law has undermined the sovereignty of Parliament in certain areas of law.

****

4

European Law

Recent history

Since January 1st 1973, when the United Kingdom joined what was then the European Economic Community, set up by the Treaty of Rome in 1957, European law has gained an ever greater significance. Currently, there are 28 (at 2015) member states in the European Union. The European Union is a vast and complex organisation. Changes were made to the EU and European Institutions to cope with the EU's expanded membership through the intended passing of a new European Constitution. The constitution within Part 1 contained wide raging reforms, *inter alia*:

- explicitly stating that EU law had priority over domestic law of Member States
- the constitution would be the highest form of law
- EU legal instruments would be reclassified to provide a clear hierarchy distinguishing between administrative and legislative forms
- The EU would have stronger political profile with the creation of a Commission President and Minister of Foreign Affairs
- The number of commissioners would be reduced to two-thirds the number of Member States
- The European parliament would be restricted to 750 members and its legislative role would be increased

- The president of the European Council would be appointed for two and a half years rather than six months
- The system of voting within the European Council would be changed.

Part 2 of the European Constitution contained a Charter of Fundamental Rights. These provisions covered:

- civil rights
- political rights
- economic rights
- social rights.

However, voters in England and France rejected the European Constitution. As a result a treaty, signed in Lisbon in 2007, was drawn up to replace the draft European Constitution. The Lisbon Treaty was initially rejected by Irish voters in a referendum on 12th June 2008. Under EU rules, the treaty could not enter into force if any of the 27 member states failed to ratify it. The treaty was eventually ratified by all 27 (as was) Member States in November 2009 and came into force on December 1st 2009. The Lisbon Treaty was ratified in the UK on 19th June 2008 under the European Union Amendment Act 2008.

Whereas the Constitution attempted to replace all earlier EU treaties and start afresh, the new treaty merely amends the Treaty on European Union and the Treaty establishing the European Union without replacing them. It provides the Union with a legal framework and tools necessary to meet future challenges and respond to citizen demands. The Lisbon treaty contains many of the changes that the Constitution attempted to introduce.

The main institutions which exercise the functions of the EU are:

- The Council of the European Union
- The Commission of the EU
- The Council of Ministers
- The European Parliament
- The European Court of Justice
- The European Central Bank

There are a number of ancillary bodies, the Economic and Social Committee being the most important.

The Council of Ministers

The government of each nation in the EU will send a representative to the Council. Usually the minister responsible for a particular area under discussion will attend. Twice a year, government heads meet in the European Council or Summit to discuss matters of policy. The member states take it in turns to provide the President of the Council, each for a six-month period. To assist with the day-to-day work of the council there is a committee of permanent representatives known as the *coreper*.

The Commission

The Commission consists of up to 30 Commissioners who are supposed to act independently. They are appointed for a five-year term and will head a specific department during their tenure. The Commission has several functions, proposing policies and presenting drafts of legislation to the Council. The Commission is also the 'guardian' of treaties. It ensures that treaty provisions adopted by the Council are properly implemented. It is also responsible for the administration of the Union.

The Assembly

The Assembly advises the Council and the Commission on economic matters. It is made up of representatives of influential interest groups such as farmers, employees and manufacturers. The Assembly must be consulted on proposed Union measures and has considerable influence on the decision making process.

The Court of Justice of the European Union

The Court of Justice of the European Union consists of three courts:

- The European Court of Justice (The ECJ)
- The General Court
- Civil Service Tribunal

The European Court of Justice

The court of primary importance is the European Court of Justice. The function of the European Court of Justice is set out in Article 220 of the Treaty of Rome. This states that ' the Court must ensure that in the interpretation and application of the treaty the law is observed'.

The Court sits in Luxembourg and has 28 judges, one from each member state. Each judge is appointed for a term of six years and can be further reappointed. The Court is assisted by nine Advocates General who are also appointed for six years. Each case brought before the EU Court of Justice is given to an Advocates General whose task is to research all the appropriate legal points and to present a reasoned conclusion on cases to the Court.

The Courts main task is to ensure that the law is applied uniformly in all member states. It will hear cases to decide whether member states have failed to fulfil obligations under the Treaties. Such actions are usually initiated by the European Commission, although they can be started by another Member State.

The Court will also hear references from national courts for preliminary rulings on points of European law. Rulings made by the European Court of Justice are then binding on all Member States. This ensures that the law is uniform throughout Member States.

A request for a preliminary ruling is made under Article 234 of the Treaty of Rome. This states:

'the Court of Justice shall have jurisdiction to give preliminary rulings concerning:

a) the interpretation of Treaties;
b) the validity and interpretation of Acts of the Institution of the Union;
c) the interpretation of the statutes of bodies established by an Act of the Council, where those statutes so provide.

Article 234 goes on to state that where there is no appeal from the national court within the national system, then courts must refer points of European law to the European Court of justice.

If this is applied to the court system in England and Wales, this means that the Supreme Court must refer questions of European law, as it is the highest appeal court in our legal system. However, the Court of Appeal does not have to refer questions.

However, even courts at the bottom of the system can refer questions of law under Article 234 if they feel that a preliminary ruling is necessary to enable a judgement in a particular case to be given. The European Court will not decide such a case only make a preliminary ruling and then refer the case back to the court in question.

Discretionary referrals

The Court of Appeal set out its approach to discretionary referrals in the case of Bulmer v Bollinger (1974). The guidelines are as follows:

- Guidance on a point of law must be necessary to come to a decision in a case
- There is no need to refer a question which has already been decided by the European Union in a previous case
- There is no need to refer a point which is reasonably clear and free from doubt
- The court must consider all the circumstances of the case
- The English court retains the discretion on whether to refer or not

The Court of First Instance

This was set up in 1988 to relieve the European Court of Justice of some of its workload. It is now known as the General Court following changes made by the Lisbon Treaty. In addition, a Civil Service Tribunal hears cases between European institutions and their employees.

The Lisbon Treaty also officially recognised the European Central Bank based in Germany as an institution of the European union. It is responsible for organising and co-ordinating both the monetary and economic policy of the Member States of the European Union that have adopted the Euro, the single European Currency. It is independently responsible for keeping inflation under control and setting interest rates within the Eurozone.

Regulations

Under Article 249 of the Treaty of Rome, the European Union has the power to issue regulations which are binding in every respect and directly applicable to every Member state. Such regulations do not have to be adopted by Member States as they automatically become law in each member country.

Directives

Directives are the main way in which harmonisation of laws within Member states is achieved. There have been directives covering a whole range of topics, such as company law, banking, insurance employment and consumer law. As with regulations, Article 249 of the Treaty of Rome gives the power to the Union to issue directives. Article 249 states directives:

' bind any Member state to which they are addressed as to the result to be achieved, while leaving to domestic agencies a competence as to form and means'

This means that Member states will pass their own laws to bring directives into effect. The usual method of implementing directives in the United Kingdom is by Statutory Instrument. One key example of this was the Unfair Terms in Consumer Contracts Regulations 1994. The time-frame for implementation is set by the European Commission.

Where Member states have not implemented a directive within the time set out by the Commission, the European Court of Justice has developed the concept of 'direct effect'. This means that a directive may be directly enforceable by an individual or by a member state. This will be the case even though a Member state has not implemented the directive or has implemented it incorrectly. The main point here is that the individual who is affected only has rights against the state. This is because of the concepts of vertical and horizontal effect.

Vertical effect

Vertical direct effect was illustrated effectively in the case of Marshall v Southampton and South West Area health Authority (1986). The facts were that Miss Marshall was required to retire from her post at the age of 62. Men doing the same work did not have to retire until the age of 65. Under the Sex Discrimination Act 1976 in English Law, this was not discriminatory. However, Miss Marshall succeeded in her action for unfair dismissal by relying on the Equal Treatment Directive 76/207. This directive had not been fully implemented in the United Kingdom but the European Court of Justice held that it was sufficiently clear and imposed obligations on a Member State. This ruling allowed Miss Marshall to succeed in her action against her employers because they were an arm of the state, i.e. they were considered as part of the state. The directive had vertical effect allowing her to rely on it to take action against them. The concept of state is quite wide, as it was ruled by the European Court of Justice in Foster v British Gas plc (1990) that the state was:

'a body, whatever its legal form, which has been made responsible, pursuant to a measure adopted by the State, for providing a public service under the control of the State and has for that purpose* *special powers beyond those which result from the normal rules applicable in relations between individuals'*.

Horizontal direct effect

Directives which have not been implemented do not give an individual any rights against other people. As seen they are only applicable in cases against the state.

The conflict between European law and national law

Inevitably there will be conflict between national and European law. European law takes precedence over national law. This was first established in Van Gend en Loos (1963) which involved a conflict of Dutch law and European law on customs duty. The Dutch Government argued that the European Court of Justice had no jurisdiction to decide whether European law would prevail over Dutch law. However, the European Court rejected this argument. In Costa v ENEL (1964) the European Court decided that even if there was a later national law this did not take precedence over EU law.

****

5

Statutory Interpretation of the Law

In many cases, there are disputes over the meaning of Acts of Parliament. Although Acts will have interpretive sections allowing for broader interpretations of the Act there is, in many cases, still confusion.

In cases such as the above it is the courts role to interpret the Act and decide the exact meaning of a particular word, group of words or a phrase. The reasons why a meaning can be unclear are many and include the fact that broad terms have been used to cover several possibilities, there is ambiguity, error in drafting, new developments rendering older Acts of Parliament obsolete, changes in the use of language and so on. For all these reasons and more, sometimes the courts are called on to interpret an Act.

Literal approach versus Purposive approach

One of the major problems concerning statutory interpretation is that of whether the judge in a case should take each word in an Act and interpret it literally or whether he/she should go beyond the literal meaning and take a more purposive approach, accept that words cannot cover all situations and look at the facts of the case more closely. In English law judges have not been able to agree on which approach to adopt. However, over the years they have developed three different rules of interpretation:

- The literal rule
- The golden rule

- The mischief rule

We will discuss each one in turn.

The literal rule

Under this rule courts will give words their plain, ordinary or literal meaning, even if the end result of such an interpretation is undesirable and not very sensible. This idea was expressed by Lord Esher in R v Judge of the City of London Court (1892) when he said:

' if the words of an Act are clear then you must follow them even though they lead to a manifest absurdity. The court has nothing to do with the question whether the legislature has committed an absurdity'.

The rule above has been used since the early nineteenth century and in many cases the outcome has been nonsense.

The golden rule

This rule is a modification of the literal rule. The golden rule starts by looking at the literal meaning but the court is then allowed to arrive at an interpretation which avoids absurdity.

The mischief rule

This rule gives the judge more discretion than the literal or golden rules. The definition of the mischief rule comes from the Heydon's case (1584) where it was said that there were four points the court should consider. These (couched in the original language) were:

1. What was the common law before the making of the Act?
2. What was the mischief and defect for which the common law did not provide?
3. What was the remedy the Parliament hath resolved and appointed to cure the disease of the commonwealth?
4. The true reason of the remedy.
   Then the office of all judges is always to make such construction as shall suppress the mischief and advance the remedy.

Under this rule therefore, the court should look to see what the law was before the Act was passed in order to discover what gap, or 'mischief' the Act was intended to cover. The court should then interpret the Act in such a way that the gap is covered.

Rules of language

Even the literal rule does not take cases in complete isolation. Other words in the Act must be looked at to see if they affect the word or phrase which is in dispute. In looking at other words the courts have developed a set of rules:

- The *ejusdem generis* rule
- The express mention of one thing excludes others
- A word is known by the company it keeps

The *ejusdem generis* rule

This rule states that where there is a list of words followed by general words, then the general words are limited to the same kind of items as the specific words. If we look at the case of *Powell v Kempton park Racecourse* (1899) the defendant was charged with 'keeping a house, an office, room or other place for betting'. He had been operating betting at what was known as Tattersall's Ring, which is outside. The court decided that the general words 'other place' had to refer to indoor places since all words in the list were indoor places so the defendant was not guilty.

There must be at least two specific words in a list for this rule to operate.

Expressio Unius Exclusio Alterius (the mention of one thing excludes others

Where there is a list of words which is not followed by general words, then the Act applies only to the items in the list. In *Tempest v Kilner* (1846) the court had to consider whether the Statute of Frauds 1677 (which required a contract for the sale of goods, wares and merchandise, of more than £10 to be evidenced in writing) applied to a contract for the sale of stocks and shares. The list 'goods, wares and merchandise, was not followed by any general words, so the court decided that only contracts for three types of things were affected by the statute: because the stocks and shares were not mentioned they were not caught by the statute.

NOSCITUR A SOCIIS (a word is known by the company it keeps)

This means that the words must be looked at in context and interpreted accordingly. It involves looking at words in the same section or other section of the Act. One case which illustrates this is *Inland Revenue Commissioners v Frere* (1965) where the section set out rules for 'interest, annuities or other annual interest'. The first use of the word 'interest' on its own could have meant any interest paid, whether daily, monthly or annually. Because of the words 'other annual interest' in the section, the court decided that 'interest' only meant annual interest.

Presumptions

The courts will also make certain presumptions about the law. If the statute clearly states the opposite, then the presumption will not apply and it is said that the presumption is rebutted. The most important presumptions are: a presumption against a change in the common law, i.e. a presumption that the common law has not changed unless Parliament has changed it in an Act; a presumption that *mens rea* is required in a criminal case. The basic common law rule is that no-one can be convicted of a crime unless it is shown that they had the intention to commit it.

There will also be a presumption that the Crown is not bound by any statute unless the statute expressly says so. There will be a presumption that legislation does not apply retrospectively.

Unified approach to interpretation

Looking at all these approaches the question is raised, how do they all fit together. The unified approach, according to Sir Rupert Cross, is thus:

1. A judge should start by using the grammatical and ordinary or, where appropriate, technical meaning of the words in the general context of the statute.
2. If the judge considers that this would produce an absurd result, then he may apply any secondary meaning, which the words are capable of bearing.
3. The judge may read in words which he considers to be necessarily implied by the words which are in the statute, and he has a limited power to add to, alter or ignore words

in order to prevent a provision from being unintelligible, unworkable or absurd.

4. In applying these rules the judge may resort to the various aids and presumptions.

The purposive approach

Using this approach, judges will decide what they believe Parliament meant to achieve. The major exponent of this approach was Lord Denning. In the case of Magor and St Mellons v Newport Corporation (1950) he said:

' We sit here to find out the intention of Parliament and carry it out, and we do this better by filling in the gaps and making sense of the enactment than by opening it up to destructive analysis'.

There have been many criticisms of the purposive approach, with judges stating that it is up to the courts not to interpret legislation but to follow the enactment. If any amendments need to be made they should be made by amending the Act.

****

6

The Legal Profession

In the English Legal System, there are two types of lawyers, Barristers and Solicitors.

The Law Society oversees the activities of solicitors as well as the legal profession as a whole. The General Council of the Bar oversees Barristers.

Solicitors

To become a solicitor it is usual to either have a law degree or have completed an extra year of law if the degree is a non-law degree. This is called the Common Professional Examination.

When the course has been completed successfully the student is still not a solicitor. A training contract must be obtained from a firm of solicitors and two years work must be completed. This training period can also be undertaken in other legal organisations such as the Crown Prosecution Service, or the legal department of a local authority. During the training period he or she will have to undertake their own work and complete a 20 day Professional Skills Course after which time the person will be admitted as a solicitor by the Law Society. Even after qualifying, solicitors have to attend continuing education to keep their skills up to date.

There is a non-graduate route to become a solicitor for mature candidates but the process takes longer to complete.

Solicitors who qualify will either work in private practice in a solicitors firm, or can work for the Crown Prosecution Service or for a local authority or government department. Some will become legal advisors to big companies.

Solicitors will work in sole practices or partnerships and the type of work carried out will be varied depending largely on the specialism of the firm. A small firm will usually cover a whole range of matters from housing, family, conveyancing and business matters. It is usual for a solicitor to specialise in a particular area.

All solicitors can act as advocates in the Magistrates Court. After 1986 solicitors can appear in a High Court to make a statement after a case has been settled.

Complaints against solicitors

A client can sue a solicitor for negligence in and out of court work. One case where this happened was Griffiths v Dawson (1993) where solicitors for the plaintiff failed to make a correct application in divorce proceedings against her husband. As a result of this the plaintiff lost financially and the solicitors were ordered to pay £21,000 compensation.

Solicitors Regulation Authority
Complaints about solicitors are handled by the Solicitors Regulation Authority and The Legal Ombudsman.

Barristers
Collectively, barristers are referred to as 'the Bar' and they are controlled by their own professional body-the General Council of

the Bar. All barristers must also be a member of one of the four Inns of Court, Lincolns Inn, Inner Temple, Middle Temple and Gray's Inn all of which are situated near the Royal Courts of Justice in London.

Entry to the Bar is usually degree based although a small number of mature entrants can qualify. As with solicitor's graduates with a non-law degree can take a one-year course for the Common Professional Examination in the core subjects in order to qualify as a barrister. All student barristers must pass the Bar Vocational Course which emphasises the practical skills of drafting pleadings for use in court negotiation and advocacy.

All student barristers must join one of the four Inns of Court. Until 1997 it was mandatory to dine there 12 times before being called to the Bar. However, students may now attend in a different way, such as a weekend residential course.

After being called to the Bar a Barrister must complete a practical stage of the training called pupillage. This is on-the-job training where the trainee barrister becomes a pupil to a qualified barrister. This involves shadowing the barrister and can be with the same barrister for 12 months or with two barristers for six months each. There is also a requirement to take part in ongoing continuing education organised by the Bar Council. After the first six months of pupillage barristers can appear on their own in court.

Barristers practicing at the Bar are self-employed but share the administrative expenses of a set of chambers. Most sets of chambers comprise 15-29 barristers. They will employ a clerk as an administrator. The majority of barristers will concentrate on advocacy, although there are some who will specialise.

Originally, it was necessary for anyone who wanted to instruct a barrister to go to a solicitor first. The solicitor would then brief the barrister. After September 2004, it has been possible for anyone to contact barristers direct. However, direct access is still not allowed for criminal work or family work.

Barristers can be employed direct (the employed bar) working for example, for the Crown Prosecution Service and can represent in court.

Queen's Counsel

After a Barrister or solicitor has served at least 16 years with an advocacy qualification, it is then possible to become a Queens Counsel (QC). About 10% of the Bar are Queens Counsel and it is known as 'taking silk'. QC's usually take on complicated, high profile cases. Until 2004 Queen's Counsel were appointed by the Lord Chancellor. After 2004, selection is by a panel chaired by a non-lawyer. Selection is by interview and applicants can provide references.

Complaints against barristers

Where a barrister receives a brief from a solicitor he or she does not enter into a contract with a client and so cannot sue if fees are not paid. Likewise the client cannot sue for breach of contract. However, they can be sued for negligence. In the case Saif Ali v Sydney Mitchell and Co (1990) it was held that a barrister could be sued for negligence in respect of written advice and opinions. In that particular case a barrister had given wrong advice on who to sue, with the result that the claimant was too late to start proceedings against the right person.

Solicitors and barristers summarised

	Solicitors	Barristers
Professional body	Law Society	Bar Council
Basic qualifications	Law degree or non-law degree with one years Common Professional Exam	Law degree or non-law degree with one years Common Professional Exam
Vocational training	Legal practice course	Bar vocational course
Practical training	Training contract	Pupillage
Methods of working	Firm of partners or sole practitioner	Self-employed Practicing in Chambers
Rights of audience	Normally only County Court and Magistrates Court	All courts
Relationship with client	Contractual	Normally through solicitor but Accountants and Surveyors can Brief barristers Directly
Liability	Liable in contract and tort to clients may also be liable to others affected by negligence	No contractual liability but liable for negligence

The Judiciary

Collectively, judges are known as the judiciary. The head of the Judiciary is the Lord Chancellor.

Types of judges

Superior judges

Superior judges are those in the high court and above. These are (from top to bottom):

- The 12 justices of the Supreme Court
- The Lords Justices of Appeal in the Court of Appeal
- Master of the Rolls (Court of Appeal Civil Division)
- Lord Justice of Appeal-Court of Appeal
- High Court Judges (known as puisne judges) who sit in the three divisions of the High Court

Specific posts heading the different divisions of the Court of Appeal and the High Court are:

- The Lord Chief Justice, who is the president of the Criminal Division of the Court of Appeal and the senior judge in the Queens Bench Division of the High Court
- The Master of the Rolls who is president of the Civil Division of the Court of Appeal
- The President of the Family Division of the High Court
- The Vice Chancellor of the Chancery Division of the High Court

Inferior judges

The inferior judges are:

- Circuit judges who sit in both the Crown Court and the County Court
- Recorders who are part-time judges sitting usually in the Crown Court though some may be assigned to the County Court

- District judges who hear small claims and other matters in the County Court
- District judges (Magistrates Court) who sit in Magistrates Courts in the major towns and cities

To become a judge at any level it is necessary to have qualified as a barrister or solicitor. It is not essential to have practiced, as the Courts and Legal Services Act 1990 provided for academic lawyers to be appointed.

Lords Justices of Appeal

Lords Justices of Appeal must have a 10-year High Court Qualification or be an existing High Court Judge.

High Court Judges

To be eligible to be a High Court Judge it is necessary either to have had the right to practice in the High Court for 10 years or more or to have been a Circuit Judge for at least 2 years. New qualifications give solicitors the chance to become High Court Judges. It is also possible for academic lawyers who have not practiced as barristers or solicitors to be appointed.

Circuit judges

To become a circuit judge a candidate can either have had rights of audience for 10 years or more in either the Crown Court or County Court or to have been a recorder. The Courts and Legal Services Act 1990 also allows for promotion after being a district judge, stipendiary magistrate or chairman of an employment tribunal for at least three years.

Recorders

A Recorder is a part-time post. The applicant must have practiced as a barrister or solicitor for at least 10 years.

District judges

District judges need a seven year general qualification. They are appointed from either barristers or solicitors. District judges in the Magistrates Court need the same qualification.

Law Officers

There is a law office within government that advises on matters of law that affects government. There are two law officers: the Attorney General and the Solicitor General. Both are members of the government of the day and are appointed by the Prime Minister. Both will usually be Members of the House of Commons. The Attorney General appoints the Director of Public Prosecutions, who heads the Crown Prosecution Service.

The Attorney General

The Attorney General is the Government's chief legal advisor. He is not a member of the main cabinet. He will advise government on legislative proposals and on criminal proceedings which have a political or public element. He is also responsible for major litigation which involves the government.

The Attorney General is appointed from those members of Parliament who are barristers and he can represent the government in court proceedings. He is the head of the English Bar but cannot practice privately as a barrister.

The Attorney General's consent is required before a prosecution can commence in certain cases such as corruption, possessing explosive substances and hijacking. He can grant immunity from prosecution and can stop proceedings for an indictable offence. He can also instruct the Director of Public Prosecutions to take over any private prosecution.

The Attorney General has the right to refer any criminal cases to the Court of Appeal (Criminal Division) for a point of law to be considered following an acquittal in the Crown Court and he can appeal against a sentence which is considered too lenient.

The Solicitor General

The Solicitor General acts as a deputy to the Attorney General.

The Director of Public Prosecutions

The DPP's duties are set out in the Prosecution of Offences Act 1985, which created the Crown Prosecution Service. The DPP must be a barrister or solicitor of at least 10 years standing. The appointment is made by the Attorney General to whom the DPP is accountable. The main function of the DPP is to head the Crown Prosecution Service. The other functions are set out in the Prosecution of Offences Act 1985, which are:

- To take over the conduct of all criminal proceedings instituted by the police
- To institute and oversee the conduct of criminal proceedings where the importance of difficulty of the proceedings makes this appropriate
- To take over the conduct of binding over proceedings brought by the police

- To give advice to police forces on all matters relating to criminal offences
- To appear for the prosecution in certain appeals

Magistrates

Magistrates are trained, unpaid members of their local community, who work part-time and deal with less serious criminal cases, such as minor theft, criminal damage, public disorder and motoring offences.

Magistrates' Court

Virtually all criminal court cases start in a magistrates' court, and more than 90 per cent will be completed there. The more serious offences are passed on to the Crown Court, either for sentencing after the defendant has been found guilty in a magistrates' court, or for full trial with a judge and jury.

Magistrates deal with three kinds of cases:

Summary offences. These are less serious cases, such as motoring offences and minor assaults, where the defendant is not usually entitled to trial by jury. They are generally disposed of in magistrates' courts.

Either-way offences. As the name implies, these can be dealt with either by magistrates or before a judge and jury at the Crown Court. Such offences include theft and handling stolen goods. A defendant can insist on their right to trial in the Crown Court. Magistrates can also decide that a case is so serious that it should be dealt with in the Crown Court – which can impose tougher sentences if the defendant is found guilty.

Indictable-only offences, such as murder, manslaughter, rape and robbery. These must be heard at a Crown Court. If the case is indictable-only, the magistrates' court will generally decide whether to grant bail, consider other legal issues such as reporting restrictions, and then pass the case on to the Crown Court.

If the case is to be dealt within a magistrates' court, the defendant(s) are asked to enter a plea. If they plead guilty or are later found to be guilty, the magistrates can impose a sentence, generally of up to six months' imprisonment for a single offence (12 months in total), or a fine, generally of up to £5,000. If found not guilty ('acquitted'), defendants are judged innocent in the eyes of the law and will be free to go – provided there are no other cases against them outstanding. Cases are either heard by two or three magistrates or by one district judge.

Who are magistrates?

Justices of the Peace, as they are also known, are local people who volunteer their services. They do not require formal legal qualifications, but will have undertaken a training programme, including court and prison visits, to develop the necessary skills. They are given legal and procedural advice by qualified clerks.

District judges are legally qualified, paid, full-time professionals and are usually based in the larger cities. They normally hear the more complex or sensitive cases. There are approximately 23,000 magistrates, 140 district judges and 170 deputy district judges operating in the roughly 330 magistrates' courts throughout England and Wales.

Justices' Clerks

Because magistrates do not need to have legal qualifications, they are advised in court on matters of law, practice and procedure. This advice is provided by Justices' Clerks and Assistant Justices' Clerks.

Magistrates in the criminal court

Over 95 per cent of all criminal cases are dealt with in the magistrates' court.

Magistrates hear less serious criminal cases including motoring offences, commit to higher courts serious cases such as rape and murder, consider bail applications, deal with fine enforcement and grant search warrant and right of entry applications. They may also consider cases where people have not paid their council tax, their vehicle excise licence or TV licences.

All magistrates sit in adult criminal courts as panels of three, mixed in gender, age, ethnicity etc whenever possible to bring a broad experience of life to the bench. All three have equal decision-making powers but only one, the chairman will speak in court and preside over the proceedings. The two magistrates sitting either side are referred to as wingers.

Most of the cases are brought to court by the Crown Prosecution Service (CPS) but there are other prosecution agencies such as RSPCA, Environment Agency, Department of Work and Pensions, English Nature etc.

Where a defendant pleads not guilty a trial will be held where the magistrates listen to, and sometimes see, evidence presented by both the prosecution and defence, decide on agreed facts and facts in dispute and consider whether the case has been proved beyond reasonable doubt.

Having found someone guilty or when someone has pleaded, the magistrates proceed to sentence using a structured decision making process and sentencing guidelines which set out the expected penalty for typical offences. They will also take note of case law and any practice directions from the higher courts and are advised in court by a legally qualified adviser.

For a single criminal offence committed by an adult, a magistrate's sentencing powers include the imposition of fines, Community Payback orders, probation orders or a period of not more than six months in custody (a total of 12 months for multiple offences). Magistrates may also sit in the Crown Court with a judge to hear appeals from magistrates' courts against conviction or sentence and proceedings on committal to the Crown Court for sentence.

Magistrates in the Youth Courts

Magistrates are specially trained to sit in youth courts, where procedures are slightly more informal than in adult criminal courts – for example, magistrates will deliberately talk directly to young defendants, rather than always through their legal representative.

In criminal cases the youth court can deal with all offences committed by a juvenile (someone under 18 years old) except homicide, which has to be dealt with in a higher court. Sentences are quite different in that they specifically address the needs of young offenders. Young defendants should always be accompanied by a responsible adult when they appear in court unless they are mature enough to be considered independent of their parents.

Magistrates – Civil

Although most magistrates deal with criminal work, they also decide many civil matters, particularly in relation to family work. Magistrates' civil roles include dealing with cases such as non-payment of council tax.

Magistrates in Family Proceedings Courts

Magistrates undergo extensive training before they sit in Family Proceedings Courts where procedures are very different from the criminal courts; the court setting is much more informal and ideally takes place with parties seated around a large table. Cases – which can be both public and private – can be very emotional and upsetting for both parties.

There is usually a fair amount of reading as both parties file statements and reports. Magistrates always provide written reasons and can be assisted with extra information provided by a children's guardian, usually a specialised social worker.

****

7

Civil Cases

We have already discussed the difference between civil cases and criminal cases. Civil cases are between individuals (including companies) and criminal cases involve the state against others.

The types of disputes that can arise in civil cases are varied. The claim can be for money, from relatively small amounts to huge amounts. Contract law can be involved. An individual may be claiming compensation for injury or some other form of injustice (tort). Other types of orders sought may be for injunctions to prevent someone from doing something or the winding up of a company or divorce following a failed marriage. Civil cases are of a wide variety. In this chapter we discuss the workings of the civil courts.

Taking a case to court is expensive unless the party to a case is prepared to go down the do-it-yourself route. However, prior to going to court it is expected by the courts that some form of negotiation has taken place. Failure to do so is looked at in a dim light by any judge.

Commencing a court case in the county courts

The civil court system has undergone significant reform since the Woolf Report of 1999. Parties to a case are encouraged to give information to each other to prevent the need to go to court in the first place. This is seen as a way of ensuring that the court system does not get clogged up with unnecessary cases. Before an action is commenced and a claim is issued, a pre-action protocol should be followed. This, basically, is a list of things that should be done and if the parties to a case or potential case do not follow a procedure and give the required information to the other party, they may be liable for certain costs if they then make a court claim.

This information will usually be in the form of a letter explaining how the claim has arisen, why it is claimed that the other party is at fault, details of the injury or other damage and anything else relevant to the case. The defendant is then given three months to respond and investigate the claim admitting or denying the claim. If any other evidence is needed, such as expert evidence then the parties should agree on one expert. If this does not solve matters then it may still be necessary to go to court.

Commencing a court case

Which court?

If a decision has been made to go to court then the question will be which court? As discussed, the two courts which hear civil cases are the county court and the high court. For cases where the claim is for £15,000 or less, the case must be started in the county court. For claims larger than this amount the High court or county court can be used. There are however, some restrictions laid down as to the use of courts in the High Court and County Courts Jurisdiction Order 1991. These are that personal injury cases for less than £50,000 must be started in the county court and defamation actions must commence in the High Court.

The main consideration when commencing a claim over £15,000 is how complex the case is going to be. If it is fairly straightforward then it should commence in the county court if it is complex then the High Court should be used.

Issuing a claim against another party

If the county court is to be used, then the claim can be issued in any of the county courts in the country. If the High Court is to be used then you can go to one of the 20 District Registries or the main court in London. You will need to use a claim form called an 'N1'. The court office will supply notes on how to fill in the form. There is a fee for commencing the case and the courts will advise you of this.

Defending a claim

When a claim form is received by a defendant there are several alternatives courses of action. The defendant can admit the claim and settle. When this happens the case ends. If the claim is defended he or she may serve an acknowledgement of service (form N9) or a defence to the court within 14 days of receiving the claim. If only an acknowledgement of service is sent then the defendant has an extra 14 days to serve the defence.

If the defendant does not respond at all, the claimant can ask the court to make an order that the defendant pays the monies owed and also costs of the claim. This is called an order in default. If the case is defended then the court will allocate the case to the most suitable 'track'.

The decision on which track to be used is made by the District Judge in the county court or the Master (a procedural judge) in the High Court. The tracks are:

- The small claims track. This is normally used for disputes under £5,000, except for personal injury and housing cases where the limit is lower, usually £1,000
- The fast track. This is normally used for straightforward disputes of £5,000-£25,000.
- The multi-track. This is for cases over £25,000 or for complex cases under this amount.

Both parties will be sent an allocation questionnaire in order to assist the judge in deciding which track to allocate the case to. Judge can also make a decision to transfer cases from one court to another.

The Small claims track

As stated, the small claims track deals with cases of £5,000 or under. People are encouraged to take their own cases so that costs are kept to a minimum. The actual process of commencing a claim is relatively simple, being paper driven. Most major towns will have a county court and addresses can be found in libraries or on the internet. These courts can hear nearly all civil cases, the main types being contract and tort cases, cases for recovery of land, disputes over partnerships, trusts and inheritance up to £30,000, divorce cases, bankruptcy, admiralty cases and matters under the Race Relations Act 1976. The county court can try small claims, fast track and multi track cases. Cases will almost always be heard in open court and members of the public are entitled to attend. The exceptions to this are matters of a more personal nature such as family matters. Cases are heard by circuit judges.

Fast-track cases

Cases of between £5000 and £25,000 are allocated to the fast track. Personal injury cases and housing cases of between £1000 and

£15,000 are also heard fast-track. Fast-track means that the court will set out a very rigid timetable for the pre-trial matters. Once a case is set down for hearing the aim is for the case to be heard within 30 weeks.

The actual trial will be heard by a circuit judge and the pre-trial hearing will last no longer than one day.

Multi-track cases

Claims for more than £25,000 are normally allocated to the multi-track. If the case was commenced in a county court then it will usually be heard there, although it can be sent to the High Court, especially if the claim is over £50,000.

The High Court

This court is based in London but has branches in 26 towns and cities throughout England and Wales. It has the power to hear any civil case and consists of three divisions each of which specialises in hearing a specific type of case: The Queens Bench Division, The Chancery Division and the Family Division.

The single family court

Since its introduction on 22nd of April 2014, the single Family Court deals with all family proceedings, except for a limited number of matters exclusively reserved to the High Court

How does the new single Family Court work?

The single Family Court provides court users with effective access to justice while seeking ways to improve the efficiency of the justice system as a whole. A single Family Court will aim to allow magistrates, legal advisers and the judiciary to work more closely together. Lay magistrates and all levels of judges will be able to sit in the Family Court. The changes mean that most proceedings will now be issued by the Family Court and cases will be allocated as soon as possible to the appropriate level of judge.

This means that cases will no longer need to be transferred between the old tiers of court. For families who need to use the court, this will help reduce delay and wherever possible, ensure greater continuity in who hears the case.

There are four levels of Family Court judges working in the one court with each level of judiciary reflecting the varying complexity of cases. Lay Magistrates, District Judges, Circuit Judges, and High Court judges will be housed in the same Court Building. This new structure should allow a more effective and efficient use of all judges' time.

Each Designated Family Centre will have at least one Designated Family Judge who will be responsible for the administrative running of the Family Court.

There will be a 'gatekeeping team' at each Family Court who will determine to which level of Judge a particular case will be allocated (a Lay Magistrate, a District Judges, a Circuit Judges or a High Court judge)

Magistrates are able to deal with all the straightforward family cases: care cases and private law contact cases.

Magistrates do not deal with anything more legally complex, such as serious abuse, possibly capacity issues (where the Official Solicitor is involved) and anything with a foreign element.

The Queens Bench Division

The President of the Queens Bench Division is the Lord Chief Justice with up to 70 judges sitting in this division. It deals with contract and tort cases where the amount being claimed exceeds £50,000. As we have seen, a claimant can start an action for £15,000 and above. The High Court will only deal with multi-track cases. There is a right to jury in cases for fraud, libel, slander, malicious prosecution and false imprisonment cases. The role of the jury is discussed later in the book.

Commercial court

This is part of the Queens Bench division with specialist judges who will listen to commercial cases such as insurance and banking.

Admiralty court

This court deals with shipping and deciding such matters as collisions at sea and salvage rights. In 1998, the Technology and Construction Court was set up to deal with complex building and engineering disputes.

The Queens Bench Division also has an important supervisory function over inferior courts, and other bodies with decision-making powers, such as government ministers and local councils. The process of judicial review concerns itself with whether a decision making process has been carried out legally.

The Chancery Division

The Lord Chancellor assisted by the Vice Chancellor is the head of the Chancery Division. The main business of this division involves disputes with matters such as insolvency, the enforcement of mortgages, disputes relating to trust property, copyright and patents, intellectual property and contested probate. There is also a special companies court dealing with winding up companies.

Family division

The head of the Family Division is the President and 17 High Court Judges are assigned to this division. It hears all wardship cases and all cases relating to children under the Children Act 1989. It also deals with all other family matters, such as declarations of nullity of marriage, and grants probate in non-contentious probate cases.

The Civil Procedure Rules

From 26th April 1999, new Civil Procedure Rules came into effect. Rule 1.1 of the CPR states that the overriding objective is to enable the court to deal with cases justly. Under the CPR the terminology has changed to make the whole process more user friendly. For example, the word 'plaintiff' has been changed to claimant.

Courts should try to:

- ensure that parties in any case are on an equal footing
- Save expense
- Deal with cases in a way which is proportionate to;
  -the amount involved (avoid costs exceeding amount claimed
  -the importance of the case
  -the complexity of the case
- Ensure that the case is dealt with quickly and fairly
- Allocate an appropriate share of the courts resources.

Judges now have more control over cases than they used to, setting out timetables for cases and eliminating time wasting and actively managing cases including identifying issues at an early stage and encouraging parties to use alternative dispute resolution.

Appellate Courts

These are courts which hear appeals from lower courts. The main appellate courts are the Divisional Courts, the Court of Appeal and the Supreme Court.

Divisional Courts

Each division of the High Court has a divisional court which has the power to hear appeals from inferior courts and tribunals.

Queens Bench Divisional Court

This is the most important of the Divisional Courts and has two main functions:
1. It hears appeals by way of case stated from criminal cases decided in the Magistrates Court.
2. It has supervisory powers over inferior courts and tribunals and also over the actions and decisions of public bodies and Government ministers. This is known as Judicial Review, as previously discussed.

The Queens Bench Divisional Court also hears matters relating to unlawful detainment and the right to liberty.

Chancery Divisional Court

The Chancery Divisional Court deals with a small number of appeals, mainly tax related appeals and appeals arising from bankruptcy cases.

Family Divisional Court

This court hears appeals from the decisions of magistrates regarding family matters and orders affecting children.

Court of Appeal (Civil Division)

The Court of Appeal has two divisions, civil and criminal. There are 35 Lord Justices of Appeal. The Civil Division is the main appellate court for civil cases and it is headed by the Master-of-the-Rolls. The Court of Appeal (Civil Division) mainly hears appeals from the following courts:

- All three divisions of the High Court
- The County Court for multi-track cases
- The Immigration Appeal Tribunal
- Some tribunals

Permission to appeal is required in most cases. It can be granted by the court where the decision was made, or by the Court of Appeal. Permission to appeal is only granted where the court feels that an appeal may have some success or there is some other reason why the appeal should be heard.

Permission to appeal is not required where the liberty of an individual is at stake.

The Supreme Court

This is the final and highest court of appeal in the English legal system. It hears appeals from the Court of Appeal, the Divisional Courts and in rare cases from the High Court.

Appeal routes in civil cases

Appeals from the County Court

The appeal routes from the County Court are set out in Part 52 of the Civil Procedure Rules.

Generally:

- fast track cases dealt with by a District judge-these appeals are heard by a Circuit Judge
- For fast track cases dealt with by a circuit judge the appeal is heard by a High Court Judge
- For final decisions in multi track cases heard in the County Court the right of appeal is to the Court of Appeal

Appeals from small claims

After October 2000 appeals against decisions in small claims cases became possible. The appeal routes are the same as for fast track cases.

Appeals from the High Court

From a decision in the High Court the appeal will go to the Court of Appeal (Civil Division). In rare cases there may be a leapfrog decision to the Supreme Court.

Further appeals

From a decision of the Court of Appeal there is a further appeal to the Supreme Court but only if the Supreme Court or Court of Appeal gives its permission to appeal. If a point of European law is involved the case may be referred to the European Court of Justice. This referral can be made by an English Court.

Remedies in civil cases

The main remedy awarded by the courts is an order for financial recompense. This is termed an award of damages. The object of awarding financial damages, in contract cases, is to put the claimant in a position, as far as possible where they may have been if the breach had not occurred. This will be the same in negligence (tort) cases.

Special damages

These will be damages which can be specifically calculated. One such example may be the cost of repairing a car after a crash.

General damages

These are for areas that cannot be so readily calculated and itemised. Personal injury cases can involve pain and suffering and the amount of general damages will include the costs of future care and provision.

Nominal damages

Where a case is won but loss cannot be demonstrated the courts will be in a position to award nominal damages in recognition of an individuals rights being infringed.

Exemplary damages

These are also termed 'punitive damages'. They are damages that are intended to punish the defendant, not only compensate the claimant. Exemplary damages are not available for breach of contract and are only awarded in tort cases where they are authorised by statute, where there has been oppressive, arbitrary or unconstitutional action by servants of the government. In addition, they are awarded where the defendant intended to make a profit from the tort which would be greater than the compensation due from the tort.

Equitable remedies

The major equitable remedies are injunctions, specific performance and rescission.

Injunctions

Temporary injunctions, called interlocutory injunctions can be granted during the course of a case This is usually granted in order to preserve the status quo between then parties while the case is awaiting a full trial.

Injunctions are used in many areas of law, contract, family and employment. Breach of an injunction is a contempt of court.

Specific performance

This is a remedy only used in contract law and it is an order that a contract should only be carried out as agreed.

Rescission

This is also only available in contract cases. The aim of rescission is to return the parties to their pre-contractual position. The main ground for rescission is a misrepresentation, which caused one party to enter into a contract erroneously.

Rectification

This is a court order that a document should be altered to reflect the party's intention.

Alternative Dispute Resolution

As we have seen, using courts to solve civil cases is costly, or can be, and takes time. As a result, many people use what is knows as Alternative Dispute Resolution (ADR) in order to arrive at a solution to their problems.

In employment cases, ADR has long been used, primarily through ACAS (Advisory, Conciliation and Arbitration Service) Neutral mediators are used in some cases. However, this is only useful if there is a hope of parties to a dispute agreeing. There are a growing number of mediation services, one of the main ones being the Centre for Dispute Resolution set up in 1991.

Conciliation is similar to mediation in that there will be a third party helping to resolve the issues. Conciliators play a more active role generally than mediators.

****

8

Criminal cases

Police Organisation

Rather than having one national police force, the UK has 43 police forces. These are independently locally run police forces, designed to forge links between the police and local communities. Working alongside police officers are Community Support officers (CSO's) civilians employed by police authorities. Their powers include the ability to:

- issue fixed penalty notices for anti-social behaviour
- carry out searches and road checks
- stop and detain school truants
- deprive an individual of their liberty for up to 30 minutes until a police officer arrives, where the suspect fails to provide his name and address or it is reasonably suspected that the details provided are inaccurate.

The Serious Crime and Police Act 2005 created a national investigation agency, The Serious Organised Crime Agency (SOCA) to tackle the heads of organised crime who undertake illegal enterprises such as drug trafficking, paedophile rings and people smuggling.

Over time, there has been a general increase in recorded crime, with violent crime on the increase. The police are obviously in the front line dealing with crime as a whole. The main police powers are contained within the Police and Criminal Evidence Act (PACE) 1984 with amendments and additions made by the Criminal Justice and Public Order Act 1994 and the Criminal Justice Act 2003. PACE also provides for the codes of practice giving extra details on the procedures for stop and search, detaining, questioning and identifying suspects. These are issued by the Home Secretary.

Police powers

The police have to exercise their powers sensitively and respect the rights of the individual citizen. At the same time they must also have sufficient powers to enable them to do their job.

The law on police powers is mainly contained within the Police and Criminal Evidence Act 1984 and the associated codes of practice contained within section 66 of the act. There are six codes:

- Code A deals with the powers to stop and search
- Code B for the powers to search premises and seize property
- Code C deals with detention, treatment and questioning of subjects
- Code D deals with the rules for identification procedures
- Code E deals with the tape recording of interviews with suspects
- Code F deals with visual recording of interviews

Powers to arrest-serious arrestable offences

Some of the rules only apply to serious arrestable offences. These include murder, treason, manslaughter, rape, hijacking, kidnapping, hostage taking, drug trafficking, firearms offences and causing explosions likely to endanger life or property. Other arrestable offences may only be considered to be serious if they endanger the state or public order or cause death of a person.

Powers to stop and search

The powers of police to stop and search people or vehicles are contained in sections 1-7 of PACE. Section 1 gives police the powers to stop and search people and vehicles in a public place. A public place has a wide meaning and extends to private gardens if the police officer in question has good reason to believe that the suspect does not live at that address. To use this power under PACE the police officer must have reasonable grounds for suspecting that the person is in possession of stolen goods or prohibited articles or goods. These include knives and other weapons which can cause harm or be used in burglary or theft.

Voluntary searches

This is where a person is prepared to submit to a search voluntarily. A voluntary search can only take place where there is power to search anyway. Voluntary searches must be recorded.

Other powers to stop and search

Apart from PACE there are also other Acts of Parliament which give the police the right to stop and search in special circumstances. The Misuse of Drugs Act 1971 allows the police to search for controlled drugs and the Anti-Terrorism, Crime and Security Act 2001 gives powers to stop and search where there is reasonable suspicion of involvement in terrorism. Section 60 of the Criminal Justice and Public Order Act 1994 gives the police an additional power of the right to stop and search in anticipation of violence.

Roadside checks

Section 4 of PACE gives police the right to stop and search vehicles if there is a reasonable suspicion that a person who has committed a serious offence is at large in an area.

The power to search premises

In certain circumstances the police have the power to enter and search premises. PACE sets out most of these powers although there are other Acts which provide for this mentioned later.

The police can enter a premises without the occupiers permission if a warrant authorising that search has been obtained from a magistrate. This will normally be issued under section 8 of PACE. The magistrate must be convinced that the police have reasonable grounds for believing that a serious arrestable offence has been committed and that there is material on the premises that will be of substantial value in the investigation of the offence. Search warrants are designed to enable the element of surprise and in the process prevent valuable evidence being removed or destroyed.

A warrant must specify the premises to be searched and, as far as possible, the articles or persons to be sought. One entry only, on one occasion is authorised and entry must be at a reasonable hour unless the police can demonstrate the need to enter at another time. They are also required to identify themselves as police officers and to show the warrant on demand.

The courts have, however, held that the police do not have to follow these requirements precisely if the circumstances of the case make it appropriate to do otherwise.

Powers to enter premises without a search warrant

Police officers may enter and search premises if it is in order to arrest a person named in an arrest warrant, or to arrest someone for an arrestable offence, or to recapture an escaped prisoner. This power is set out in section 17 of PACE. Reason for the entry must be given to anyone in the premises. PACE also gives a police officer the right to enter a premises without a search warrant after an arrest if an officer has grounds to believe that there is evidence on the premises relating to the offence for which the person has just been arrested.

To prevent a breach of the peace

There is a right under common law for police to enter premises if there is a need to deal with or prevent a breach of the peace. This right applies even to private homes as was demonstrated by the case of McLeod v Commissioner of Police for the Metropolis (1994) in which the police had entered domestic premises when there was a violent quarrel taking place.

Searching with the consent of the occupier of the premises

The police may enter and search a premises without a warrant if the occupier of these premises gives them permission to do so. This consent must be given in writing and can be withdrawn.

Unlawful entry and search

If a premises is entered and searched unlawfully, where the police exceed their powers a claim for damages can be made under the tort of trespass.

Powers of arrest

Section 24 of PACE sets out the general powers of arrest, and some of these powers can be exercised by private citizens as well as the police.

Arrestable offences

An arrestable offence is:

1. Any offence for which the sentence is fixed by law. An example may be murder which has a fixed term of life imprisonment.
2. Any offence for which the maximum sentence that could be given to an adult is five years imprisonment.
3. Any other offence which Parliament has specifically made an arrestable offence.

PACE Section 24-Arrests by police and private citizens

This section allows the police or a private citizen to arrest without a warrant:

1. Anyone who is in the act of committing an arrestable offence
2. Anyone whom he has reasonable grounds for suspecting to be committing an arrestable offence
3. Anyone who has committed an arrestable offence
4. Where an arrestable offence has been committed, anyone for whom he has reasonable grounds for suspecting to be guilty of it.

The police also have the right to arrest anyone who is about to commit an arrestable offence, anyone whom he has reasonable grounds for suspecting to be about to commit an arrestable offence or where there are reasonable grounds for suspecting that an arrestable offence has been committed.

PACE Section 25

Police have further powers under section 25 to arrest for any offence where the suspects name and address cannot be discovered or that there are reasonable grounds to believe that the name and address given by the suspect are false.

Section 25 also provides powers of arrest where there are reasonable grounds for believing that arrest is necessary to prevent that person from:

- Causing physical injury to himself or others
- Suffering physical injury (i.e. suicide)
- Causing loss or damage to property
- Committing an offence against public decency
- Causing an unlawful obstruction of the highways

Section 25 also gives the police powers to arrest if the arrest is believed to be necessary to protect a child or other vulnerable person.

Other rights of arrest

The Criminal Justice and Public Order Act 1994 added an extra power of arrest to PACE. This is in section 46A of PACE and gives the police the right to arrest without a warrant anyone who has been released on police bail and fails to attend a police station at an allotted time. The Criminal Justice and Public Order Act also gives police the right to arrest for a variety of new offences in connection with collective or aggravated trespass.

Arrest for breach of the peace

The police have a right to arrest where there has been or is likely to be a breach of the peace. The conditions for arrest for breach of the peace were laid down in *Bibby v Chief Constable of Essex Police (2000)*. These are:

- There must be sufficiently real and present threat to the peace
- The threat must come from the person to be arrested
- The conduct of the person must clearly interfere with the rights of others and its natural consequence must be 'not wholly unreasonable' violence from a third party
- The conduct of the person to be arrested must be unreasonable

The right to search an arrested person

Where a person has been arrested the police have a right to search that person for anything which might be used to help an escape or anything that might be evidence relating to an offence.

Powers to detain suspect

Once a person has been arrested and taken to a police station there are rules setting out time limits as to detention. The limits will vary and are longer depending on the severity of the offence. There are also rules, contained in PACE relating to treatment of people in detention.

The general rules are that the police may detain a person for 24 hours. After this the police can detain a person for a further 12 hours but only with the permission of a senior officer. After 36 hours those detained for an ordinary arrestable offence must be released or charged. For serious offences those detained can be held for a further period but a magistrates order must be obtained and the maximum detention cannot exceed 96 hours. There is a right to representation. There is an exception under terrorism offences which allows for detention of 48 hours and up to another 12 days with the Home Secretary's permission.

Rights of detained people

Detainees must be informed of their rights. These include:

- Someone must/can be informed of the arrest
- Being told that independent legal advice is freely available and being allowed to consult with a solicitor
- Being allowed to consult the code of practice

Police interviews

Detained persons may be interviewed by the police. All interviews carried out at a police station must be tape recorded. Suspects have the right to a solicitor during questioning. If a solicitor is not asked for or is late questioning can commence. If the person is under 17 or is mentally handicapped there must be an 'appropriate adult' present during questioning.

Section 76 of PACE states that a court shall not allow statements which have been obtained through oppression to be used as evidence.

The right to silence

A defendant has the right to remain silent but inferences can be drawn from the silence and used in court. The wording of a caution given to a suspect states:

'You do not have to say anything. But it may harm your defence if you do not mentioned when questioned something which you later rely on in court. Anything you do say may be given in evidence'

Searches, fingerprints and samples

When a person is being held at a police station the police do not have an automatic right to search them. However, a custody officer has a duty to record everything a person has with them and if the custody officer thinks a search is necessary then a non-intimate search can be made. A strip search can only take place if it is necessary to remove an article which a person in detention should not be allowed to keep and there is reasonable suspicion that a person may have concealed an article. There are strict rules governing the nature of a strip search and articles of clothing that can be removed at once and in which places.

The police can take fingerprints and non-intimate body samples without the persons consent. Reasonable force can be used to obtain these if necessary. There are different rules for intimate samples. These are defined in the Criminal Justice and Public Order Act 1994 as:

a) a sample of blood, semen or other tissue, fluid, urine or public hair

b) a dental impression

c) a swab taken from a person's body orifice other than the mouth

These can only be taken by a registered medical practitioner or nurse. Samples can be retained.

Complaints against the police

People who believe that the police have acted unjustly and exceeded their powers can complain and the type of complaint will determine how it is dealt with. Minor complaints are dealt with informally and more serious complaints will be dealt with at a higher level.

The Independent Police Complaints Commission

This was set up in 2004 to supervise the handling of complaints against the police and associated staff, such as Community Support Officers. The IPCC sets down standards for the police to follow when dealing with complaints. They also monitor the way complaints are dealt with by local police forces.

The IPCC will also investigate serious issues including any accident involving death or serious injury, allegations of corruption, allegations against senior officers, allegations involving racism and allegations of perverting the course of justice.

Any member of the public can complain and complaints can be made directly to the IPCC or through organisations such as the Citizens Advice Bureau or through the Commission for Equality and Human Rights or the Youth Offending Team. It is also possible to complain through a solicitor or an MP. Where the police have committed a crime in the execution of their duties criminal action can be brought against them.

9

Hearing Criminal Cases

As the criminal law is set down by the state, bringing a prosecution for breach of criminal law is seen as the role of the state. The majority of prosecutions are brought by the Crown Prosecution Service which is the agency of the state for criminal prosecutions.

A criminal prosecution can also be brought by an individual or company although this is rare. The following is an outline of the procedure for criminal trials.

Pre-trial hearings

All criminal cases will first go to the magistrates court and, in most cases, will be referred to a higher court unless the offence is minor or the person(s) plead guilty.

Categories of criminal offences

Criminal offences are divided into three main categories as follows:

1. Summary offences. These are the least serious and are always tried in the Magistrates Court. They include nearly all driving offences, common assault and criminal damage of less than £5,000.
2. Triable either way offences. These are a middle range type offence and can include assault causing actual bodily harm. These cases can be tried either in the Magistrates Court or the Crown Court.

3. Indictable offences. These are more serious crimes such as rape or murder. All such offences must be tried at the Crown Court, the first hearing being at the Magistrates Court.

Bail

One matter to be decided pre-trial is that of bail, whether the defendant should stay in custody while awaiting trial or whether he or she should be released on bail. Being granted bail means that the person is at liberty until the next stage of the case.

The police may release a suspect on bail while they pursue their enquiries. The suspect must return to the police station at a specified date in the future. The police can also grant bail to a defendant who has been charged with an offence. In this case the person is bailed to appear at a Magistrates Court at a later date. The decision on whether to grant bail or not is made by a custody officer under section 38 of PACE. Bail can be refused if the suspects name and address cannot be ascertained or there is doubt as to the validity of information.

The principles as to when bail should be granted are contained within the Bail Act 1976. This is the key Act, starting with the assumption that an accused person should be granted bail, though this right can be limited for certain cases such as terrorism or repeat serious offences. Section 4 of the Bail Act 1976 gives a general right to bail, but this can be withdrawn if the court believes that there are grounds for believing the defendant, if released, would fail to surrender to custody, commit an offence whilst on bail or interfere with witnesses or obstruct the course of justice.

In deciding whether to grant bail the court will consider various factors:

- The nature and seriousness of the offence
- The character of the defendant and community ties
- The record of the defendant
- The strength of evidence against the defendant.

The courts have the powers to impose conditions on the granting of bail. These are similar to those granted to the police, as outlined below.

Bail sureties

The courts or police can require a surety for bail. This is another person who is willing to pay a sum of money if that person doesn't turn up to court. No money is paid until the defendant breaks bail.

If any person granted bail by the police fails to attend the next stage of the case then the police can make an arrest.

Like the courts, the police have powers to impose conditions on bail. These are contained within the Criminal Justice and Public Order Act 1994. These conditions can vary, ranging from surrender of passport to regular reporting at a police station.

If the police are not prepared to grant bail then they must bring the suspect before a magistrate's court. The magistrates can then make a decision as to whether the suspect should be released on bail.

Restrictions on bail do exist, such as terrorism cases and situations where there have been repeated serious offences.

Section 19 of the Criminal Justice Act 2003 amended the Bail Act 1976 and placed certain restrictions on bail for adult drug offenders who have tested positive for specific Class A drugs where the offender is either charged with possession or possession with intent to supply a Class A drug or the court is satisfied that there are grounds for believing that misuse of a class A drug contributed to the offence or that the offence was motivated wholly or partly by the intended misuse of a drug and the defendant has refused to participate in an assessment or follow up in relation to the dependency on Class A drugs.

The prosecution in a case can appeal against the granting of bail. This is set out in the Bail (Amendment) Act 1993.

The Crown Prosecution Service

The Crown Prosecution Service (CPS) was established by the Prosecution of Offences Act 1985 and began life in 1986. The head of the CPS is the Director of Public Prosecutions who must have been a qualified lawyer for 10 years. The DPP is appointed by the Attorney General. Under the DPP are Chief Crown Prosecutors who each head one of 42 areas. Each area is sub-divided into branches, each of which is headed by a Branch Crown prosecutor. Within branches there are lawyers and support staff that are given responsibility for cases.

The functions of the CPS involve all aspects of prosecution as outlined below:

- Deciding on what offences should be charged
- Reviewing all cases given to them by the police to see if there is sufficient evidence to proceed and whether it is in the public interest to do so
- Taking responsibility for the case
- Conducting the prosecution of cases in the Magistrates Court

- Conducting cases in the Crown Court

Once a defendant has been charged with an offence then the police role in the matter is over and the case is handed over to the CPS.

Criminal courts

The two courts which hear criminal cases are the Magistrates Court and the Crown Court. If a defendant in either one of these courts pleads guilty to a charge against them the role of the court is to pass sentence. Where the accused pleads not guilty the role of the court is to try the case and establish whether the defendant is guilty or not guilty. The burden of proof is on the prosecution who must prove the case beyond reasonable doubt. The form of trial is adversarial with prosecution and defence presenting their cases and cross-examining witnesses while the role of the judge is to be a referee, overseeing the trial and ensuring that the law is adhered to. The judge does not investigate the case.

The role of the Magistrates Court

There are about 430 Magistrates Courts in England and Wales. Magistrates Courts are local courts and they will be in almost every town whilst big cities will usually have several. Cases are heard by magistrates, who may be either qualified District Judges or unqualified lay justices. There is a legally qualified clerk attached to each court to provide assistance.

Magistrates Courts have jurisdiction in a variety of matters. They will:

- Try all summary cases

- Try any triable either way offences which it has been decided should be dealt with in the Magistrates Court
- Deal with the first hearings of all indictable offences
- Deal with other matters connected to criminal offences such as issuing warrants for bail and deciding bail applications
- Try cases in the Youth Court where the defendant is aged 10-17

The Magistrates Courts also have some civil jurisdiction including enforcing council tax demands and issuing warrants of entry and investigation to utilities such as gas and electricity, family cases, proceedings concerning the welfare of children under the Children Act 1989.

Summary Trials

Summary trials are the least serious criminal offences. They are further divided into offences on different levels ranging from level one (lowest) to level five (highest). Fines are set in accordance with each level. For level one the fine is maximum £200, level two £500, level three £1,000, level four £2,500 and level five £5,000. These fines arise from the Criminal Justice Act 1991 and are increased periodically to account for inflation. The maximum prison sentence that can be given for summary offences is six months which will shortly be increased to 15 months following the passing of the Criminal Justice Act 2003.

At the start of any summary trial the defendant will be asked whether he or she pleads guilty or not guilty. If a guilty plea is entered the case will be explained to the court and the prosecutor and defence will put their case and the magistrates will decide sentence.

If a not guilty plea is entered, the procedure is rather more complicated as the prosecutor has to provide evidence to the court and prove the case. Witnesses are called. At the end the defence can call for the case to be dismissed on lack of evidence if this is the case. The magistrates will then decide on the case, whether guilty or not guilty.

Triable either way cases

Plea before venue

Under this procedure the defendant is asked whether he pleads guilty. If the plea is guilty then there is no right to ask to go to a Crown Court although the magistrate may still decide to send him there for sentence.

If the defendant pleads not guilty then the magistrates must carry out 'mode of trial' proceedings to establish where the case will be tried. Under section 19 of the Magistrates Court Act 1980 they must consider the nature and seriousness of the case and decide a course of action. If the case involves complex cases of law it will usually be referred to the Crown Court. It will also be referred to the Crown Court if it is of a particularly serious nature and has, for example, involved organised crime or where the amount involved was particularly high, more than twice the potential fine that magistrates can levy.

In cases, rare cases, where the Attorney General, Solicitor General or Director of Public Prosecutions is the prosecutor, magistrates must abide by the wishes of the prosecutor and send the case to the Crown Court if this is what is wanted.

If magistrates accept jurisdiction, the defendant is informed that he has the right to trial by jury, in the Crown Court, but may be tried by magistrates if he so wishes. If the magistrates feel that they have insufficient powers to punish they can refer the matter to the Crown Court for sentencing.

Sending cases to the Crown Court

For indictable offences the case is automatically referred by magistrates to the Crown Court. Section 51 of the Crime and Disorder Act 1988 dictates this. For triable either way offences, magistrates will hold a plea before venue and, if the plea is not guilty, a mode of trial hearing. The decision to try the case in the Magistrates Court or the Crown Court is taken at this point.

Committal proceedings

Magistrates can commit a defendant charged with a triable either way offence for sentence in the Crown Court.

Role of the court clerk

Every bench of magistrates is assisted by a clerk who is also a legal advisor. The senior clerk in each court has to be a barrister or solicitor of at least five years standing. The role of the clerk is to guide the magistrates on questions of law, practice and procedure.

Youth courts

Youth offenders aged between 10-17 are dealt with in the Youth court which is a branch of the Magistrates court. Children under the age of 10 cannot be charged with a criminal offence. There are some exceptional cases where the case can be tried in the Crown Court if the charge is one of manslaughter or murder, rape or causing death by dangerous driving. In addition, it is possible to send a person over 14 to the Crown Court if the charge is sufficiently serious.

Appeals from the Magistrates Court

The system of appeal routes from the magistrate's court will depend on whether the appeal is on a point of law or for other reasons. The two appeal routes are the Crown Court or the Queens Bench Divisional Court.

The normal route of appeal is the Crown Court and can only be used by the defence. If the defendant has pleaded guilty then the appeal can only be against sentence. If the plea was not guilty then the appeal can be against conviction or sentence. In both cases the defendant has the automatic right to appeal.

Further appeal to the Supreme Court

From the decision of the Queens Bench Court there is a possibility of a further appeal to the Supreme Court. This can only be made if:

1. The Divisional Court certifies that a point of law of general public importance is involved.
2. The Divisional Court or the Supreme Court gives leave to appeal because the point is one which ought to be considered by the Supreme Court.

The Crown Court

The Courts Act 1971 set up the Crown Court to deal with all cases that were not tried at the Magistrates Court. The Crown Court sits in 90 different centres throughout England and Wales. There are three kinds of centre:

1. First tier-these exist in main centres throughout the country. At each court there is a High court and a Crown Court. The Crown Court is staffed by High Court Judges as well as Circuit Judges and Recorders. The court can deal with all categories of crime triable on indictment.
2. Second tier-this is a Crown Court only, but High Court judges can sit there on a regular basis to hear cases, as well as Circuit Judges and Recorders.
3. Third tier-this is staffed by Circuit judges and Recorders. The most serious cases are not usually tried here.

Preliminary matters in the Crown Court

The indictment

The indictment is a document which formally sets out charges against a defendant.

Disclosure by prosecution and defence

The Criminal Procedure and Investigations Act 1996 places a duty on both sides to make certain points of the case known to each other. The 1996 Act also imposes a duty on the defence in cases which are to be tried on indictment. After the prosecutors initial disclosure, the defence must give a written statement to the prosecution setting out:

1. the nature of the accused persons defence
2. the matters on which he takes issue with the prosecution and why he intends to take issue

3. any point of law which he wishes to take, and the case authority on which he will rely.

4.

Details of alibis and witnesses he intends to call to support the alibi. This information gives the prosecution time to carry out police checks on the witnesses.

A preliminary hearing called a 'plea and directions' hearing is held after a case has been forwarded to a Crown Court, normally within four weeks if the defendant is being held in custody and six weeks if not. The purpose of this hearing is to discover whether the plea is guilty or not guilty. All charges are read out in open court and the defendant will plead one way or the other. This is called the 'arraignment'. If the defendant pleads guilty the judge will sentence the defendant immediately, if possible. Where a defendant pleads not guilty the judge will require the defence and prosecution to identify the key issues of fact and law that are involved in the case. He will then give directions that are necessary for the organisation of the trial.

The trial

A defendant appearing at the Crown Court will usually be represented by a barrister and sometimes a solicitor. Defendants can represent themselves and can, in most cases, cross-examine witnesses although there are some cases where this cannot happen, such as sexual offences.

The order of events at a trial will depend on whether the defendant pleads guilty or not guilty. If the plea is not guilty the following will happen:

*   The jury is sworn in to try the case

- The prosecution will make an opening speech outlining the case to the jury
- The prosecution witnesses give evidence and can be cross examined by the defence-other evidence can be produced
- At the end of the prosecutions presentation the defence can state that there is no case to go to the jury: if the judge decides that this is so then he will direct the jury to acquit the defendant
- The defence may make an opening speech provided that they intend calling evidence other than the defendant
- The defence witnesses give evidence and are cross examined by the prosecution
- The prosecutor makes a closing speech pointing out the strengths of the case to the jury
- The defence makes a closing speech pointing out the weaknesses of the case
- The judge sums up the case to the jury and directs them on any law relevant to the case
- The jury retire to consider their verdict
- The jury returns and gives their verdict
- If the verdict is guilty the judge then sentences the accused, if not guilty the defendant is discharged.

It is normal, once acquitted, that the defendant cannot be re-tried. However, Under the Criminal Justice Act 2003 the double jeopardy rule was removed for serious cases if new and compelling evidence comes to light.

Appeals in criminal cases

The defendant can appeal against conviction to the Court of Appeal (Criminal Division). The appeal must be lodged verbally at the court or within 14 days of the sentence in writing. A notice of appeal must be lodged with the Court of Appeal within 28 days.

The Criminal Appeal Act 1995 states that the Court of Appeal:

a) shall allow an appeal against conviction if they think that the conviction is unsafe; and

b) shall dismiss such an appeal in any other case.

The Court of Appeal can allow an appeal and quash the conviction, vary the sentence or overturn the appeal. A re-trial can also be ordered with a new jury. The prosecution also has limited rights of appeal. In the case of jury tampering an appeal against a not guilty finding is allowed. In addition, under s 36 of the Criminal Justice Act 1972 the Attorney General can refer a point of law to the Court of Appeal. The decision does not affect the acquittal but can influence future law. Under s36 of the Criminal Justice Act 1988 the Attorney general can apply for leave to refer what is considered to be an unduly lenient sentence to the Court of Appeal for re-sentencing.

Appeals to the Supreme Court

Both prosecution and defence may appeal from the Court of Appeal to the Supreme Court. However, it is necessary to get the case certified as involving a point of law of general public importance, either from the Court of appeal or the House of Lords.

References to the European Court of Justice

In a case where a point of European law is involved it is possible for any court to make reference to the European Court of Justice under Article 177 of the Treaty of Rome.

Sentencing

Judges and magistrates have a fairly wide discretion when it comes to passing sentence on a guilty party, although they are subject to certain restrictions. Magistrates can only impose a maximum of six months imprisonment for one offence and twelve months for two. The Criminal Justice Act 2003 provides powers to increase the sentence for one offence to 12 months and two or more offences 15 months.

Judges in the Crown Court can impose up to life imprisonment for some crimes and there is no maximum figure for fines.

There are certain other restrictions placed on the Magistrates and Crown Courts by Parliament. The maximum sentence to be handed out varies depending on the crime and Parliament determines the length of sentences.

Murder carries a mandatory life sentence, whereas the judge can work within the parameters of maximum of life for other crimes such as rape and manslaughter.

When judges or magistrates pass sentence they will look at what they are trying to achieve when sentencing. Section 142 of the Criminal Justice Act 2003 sets out the purpose of sentencing for those aged 18 and over. This states that the court must have regard to:

- the punishment of offenders
- the reduction of crime
- the reform and rehabilitation of offenders
- the protection of the public

- the making of reparation by offenders to persons affected by their offences

Courts have several different types of sentences available to them. There are four main categories: custodial sentences, community sentences, fines and discharges.

Custodial sentences

This is imprisonment and is the most serious sentence that a court can pass. Prison can range from a weekend to life. Custodial sentences include:

- mandatory and discretionary life sentences
- fixed term sentences
- short term sentences
- intermittent custody
- suspended sentences

Community sentences

Prior to the Criminal Justice Act 2003, the courts had individual community sentences that they could impose on an offender. The Act created one community order under which the courts can combine any requirements that they think are necessary. These requirements include all the previous existing community sentences which become available as 'requirements' or sentences required to rehabilitate the offender, and can be attached to the sentence. The sentence is available for offenders of 16 or over. The full list of 'requirements' is set out in s 177 of the Criminal Justice Act 2003 which states:

'177 (1) Where a person aged 16 or over is convicted of an offence, the court by or before which he is convicted may make an order imposing on him any one or more of the following requirements:

a) an unpaid work requirement
b) an activity requirement
c) a programme requirement
d) a prohibited activity requirement
e) a curfew requirement
f) an exclusion requirement
g) a residence requirement
h) a mental health treatment requirement
i) a drug rehabilitation requirement
j) an alcohol treatment requirement
k) a supervision requirement
l) in the case where an offender is under 25, an attendance centre requirement.

Fines

The maximum fine in a Magistrates court is £5,000. The magistrates can impose a fine of up to £20,000 on businesses which have committed offences under various regulatory legislation such as health and safety at work.

Discharges

A discharge can be conditional or absolute. Conditional discharge means that the discharge is on condition that no further offence is committed in a set period up to three years. An absolute discharge means that no penalty has been imposed.

Other powers available to the courts

Courts can order compensation to a victim of crime. In the Magistrates court the maximum compensation is £5,000. If the defendant still has the property that he took from the victim then the court can order that it be returned. This is called a restitution order.

A court can order that a person be deprived of property that he has used to commit the offence. There is special power to order forfeiture in drug related cases. The Proceeds of Crime Act 1995 also gives the courts powers to take from criminals all profits from crime for up to six years before conviction.

Young offenders

As with adult offenders the courts have powers to order custodial sentences, fines and discharges but there are a range of different sentences available and also restrictions on what the courts can order. As far as community sentences are concerned, young offenders aged 16 or over can be given the same sentences as adults. They cannot be used for offenders under the age of 16. However, Curfew Orders can be used for those over 10 years of age. There are a number of other orders aimed at young offenders:

Attendance centre orders

This type of order is only for those under 25 and is available for all young offenders from 10 years onwards. It involves attendance at a special centre for two or three hours a week up to a maximum of 36 hours for 16-24 year olds and 24 hours for 10-15 year olds. The minimum number of hours is usually 12 but can be less for offenders under 14. The centres are run by the probation services and are usually on a Saturday afternoons. An attendance centre order cannot be made if an offender has served a period of detention previously.

Supervision orders

Section 69 of the Crime and Disorder Act 1998 created a new community order called an Action Plan order. The courts can impose this on offenders under the age of 18. The order places the offender under supervision and also sets out requirements the offender has to comply with in respect to his actions and whereabouts during a period of three months. The requirements can be any one of the following:

- To participate in set activities
- To present himself to a specified person at set times and places
- To attend at an attendance centre
- To stay away from certain places
- To comply with arrangements for his education
- To make reparation

Fines for young offenders

The maximum amount of the fine varies with the age of the offender. 10-13 year olds can only be fined a maximum of £250, 14-17 year olds £1,000. Those over 18 are subject to adult rules.

Reparation orders

A Reparation Order may be imposed on offenders under the age of 18. This order cannot be made in combination with a custodial sentence. Community Service Order, a combination order, a supervision order or an Action Plan Order. An order will require the defendant to make reparation as defined in the order:

- To a person or persons who were victims of the offence or were otherwise affected by it, or
- To the community at large

The order is for a maximum of 24 hours work and the order must be completed under supervision within three months of its imposition. An order for direct reparation to a person can only be made with that persons consent.

Discharges

These may be used for an offender of any age and are most commonly used for young first time offenders who have committed minor crimes. The courts cannot conditionally discharge an offender where a child or young offender has been warned within the previous two years, unless there are exceptional circumstances. Also, the courts cannot conditionally discharge an offender where the offender is in breach of an anti-social behaviour order or where the offender is in breach of a sex offender order.

Reprimands and warnings

These are methods with which the police can deal with young offenders without bringing them to court. There is a limit to the number of times and occasions that an offender can be cautioned.

Responsibility of parents

Parents can be bound over to keep their child under control for a set period of time up to one year. The parents must agree to this. If the child then commits an offence within this period the parents must pay a sum up to £1,000 maximum.

Where an offender under 16 is fined or ordered to pay compensation, the court must order the parents to pay. The financial situation of the parents is taken into account when assessing the amount.

Parenting orders

Parenting orders are intended to offer training and support to parents to help change their children's offending behaviour. Under a parenting order a parent can be required to attend counselling or guidance sessions for up to three months on a basis of a maximum once per week.

In addition, the parent may be required to comply with conditions imposed by the court. A court may make a parenting order where:

- The court makes a Child safety Order
- The court makes an anti-social behaviour order or sex offender order in respect of the child
- A child or young person is convicted of an offence
- A parent is convicted of an offence related to truancy under the Education Act 1996.

Offenders who are mentally ill

The law recognises, as far as it possibly can, that mentally ill offenders should receive treatment as opposed to punishment. Courts have a wide range of powers available to them when dealing with such offenders. The main extra powers available to courts are to give the offender a community sentence with a requirement that he or she attends for treatment, make a hospital order or to make a restriction order under the Mental Health Act 1983 section 41.

Under the same section, offenders with severe mental health problems can be sent to high security hospitals such as Broadmoor. Such an order can only be made by the Crown Court.

Anti-social behaviour orders

Known as ASBO's these are civil orders. They are imposed on a person who has behaved in an anti-social way. The type of behaviour termed anti-social is very wide and can include drunkenness, drug taking or causing prolonged and excessive nuisance to neighbours or the wider community.

Under an ASBO a person can be ordered not to repeat a certain anti-social behaviour or not to go to a certain place. In short it has the effect of an injunction.

There is currently a wide ranging review of Anti-Social behaviour orders following the election of the coalition government in 2011. this is because it is seen that ASBO's are largely ineffective and don't achieve their main purpose.

****

10

Juries

Juries have been in the legal system for a long time, over one thousand years. Only a small percentage of cases is tried by jury today. However, juries are used in the following courts:

- Crown Court for criminal trials on indictment
- High Court (Queens Bench Division (only for certain cases)
- County Court for similar cases to the Queens Bench Division
- Coroners Courts

The most important use of juries is in the Crown Court in criminal trials, where they decide the guilt or otherwise of the defendant. However, given that most criminal cases are decided in the Magistrates Court only about 1% of all criminal cases are tried in the Crown Court by jury.

Civil cases

Juries in civil cases are used in only limited circumstances. The present rules for when juries may be tried in civil cases are set out in section 69 of the Supreme Court Act 1981 for High Court cases, and section 66 of the County Courts Act 1984 for cases in the County Court. The Acts state that parties have the right to jury trial only in the following types of case:

- Defamation

- False imprisonment
- Malicious prosecution
- Fraud

The present qualifications to be a juror are set out in the Juries Act 1974 (as amended). To qualify for jury service a person must be:

- Aged between 18-70
- Registered as a voter
- Resident in the United Kingdom, the Channel Islands or the Isle of man for at least five years since their thirteenth birthday and must not be:
- A mentally disordered person or disqualified from jury service

Disqualification from jury service involves having a criminal record, usually one that has entailed serving a term in prison, a suspended sentence or a community sentence. In addition, anyone who is currently on bail in criminal proceedings is disqualified from sitting as a juror.

Selecting a jury

At each Crown Court there is an official who is responsible for summonsing enough jurors to try the cases to be heard in each two-week period. The official will arrange for names to be selected at random from the electoral registers for the area which the court covers. Those summonsed must notify the court of for any reason they cannot attend. All others are expected to attend for two weeks jury service. If a trial carries on for longer than two weeks then the jury will be expected to stay on longer.

Routine police checks are carried out on prospective jurors to eliminate those with unsuitable criminal backgrounds. A further check is made on a juror's background to ascertain political affiliations although this should be carried out only in exceptional circumstances and can only be carried out with the Attorney General's permission.

Juries are usually divided into groups of 15 and 12 will be selected to hear a case. Once they have been selected these jurors come into the jury box to be sworn in as jurors. At this point, before the jury has been sworn in, both the prosecution and defence have certain rights to challenge one or more of the jurors. There are two challenges that can be made and, in addition, the prosecution have a special right of 'stand by'.

These are:

- to the array
- for cause
- prosecution right to stand by jurors

To the array-this right to challenge arises from the Juries Act 1974 and it is a challenge to the whole jury on the basis that it has been chosen in an unrepresentative or biased way.

For causes-this involves challenging the right of an individual juror to sit on a jury.

Prosecution right to stand by jurors-this is a right that only the prosecution can exercise. It allows the juror who has been stood by to be put at the end of the list of potential jurors so that they will not be used unless there is a lack of jurors.

119

Juries role in criminal cases

The jury is only used at the Crown Court where the defendant pleads not guilty. The trial is presided over by a judge and the functions split between judge and jury. The judge will decide points of law and the jury decides the facts. At the end of a case, the judge can direct a jury to acquit a defendant if he feels that the prosecutions evidence does not make a case. This is called a directed acquittal.

Majority verdicts

If, after at least two hours (longer where there are several defendants) the jury have not reached a verdict the judge can call them back into the courtroom and direct them to pass a majority verdict. Where there is a full jury of 12, the verdict can be 10-2 or 11-1 either for guilty or not guilty. If the jury has fallen below 12 for any reason then only one can disagree with the verdict. A jury cannot go below nine.

The jury discussion takes place in secret and there can be no enquiry as to how the jury reached its verdict. Section 8 of the Contempt of Court Act 1981 makes disclosure of anything that happens in a jury room a contempt of court which is a criminal act.

****

11

Legal aid and advice

Many people will require legal assistance of one sort or another when either taking or defending a legal action. Lack of knowledge and difficulty in meeting costs are the two main reasons for needing assistance. One principal issue for the provision of legal services (both civil and criminal) is the quantum of public funding-as the Justice Secretary explained on 30th June 2010:

'Our legal aid system has grown to an extent that we spend more than almost anywhere else in the world. France spends £3 per head of the population, Germany £5, New Zealand £8. In England and Wales, we spend a staggering £38 per head of population.

Anther principal issue is the nature of services provided (advice, professional, representation or both) in respect of criminal and civil law.

The Legal Aid Agency
The Legal Aid Agency provides both civil and criminal legal aid and advice in England and Wales. The work of the LAA is essential to the fair, effective and efficient operation of the civil and criminal justice systems. They are a delivery organisation which commissions and procures legal aid services from providers (solicitors, barristers and the not-for-profit sector).

Governance
The Legal Aid Agency is an executive agency of the Ministry of Justice. It came into existence on 1 April 2013 following the

abolition of the Legal Services Commission as a result of the Legal Aid, Sentencing and Punishment of Offenders (LASPO) Act 2012. The Act created the new statutory office of the Director of Legal Casework. The Director will take decisions on the funding of individual cases. Processes have been put in place to ensure the Legal Aid Agency is able to demonstrate independence of decision-making. There will be an annual report published about these decisions.

Strategic objectives

The priorities of the LAA are to:

- improve casework to reduce cost, enhance control and give better customer service
- improve organisational capability to meet the challenges ahead, including developing and engaging our people
- build and maintain strong partnerships to secure quality provision and contribute fully to wider justice and Government aims

Other parts of the organisation

Public Defender Service

The Public Defender Service (PDS) is a department of the Legal Aid Agency that operates alongside private providers delivering a full range of quality services within the criminal defence market from advice and representation at the police station and magistrates courts through to advocacy in the higher courts.

Legal Aid and financial help

Legal Aid, (previously known as Public Funding) allows for state funding of legal cases in certain very limited legal and financial circumstances.

The different types of civil legal aid

There are different types of legal aid obtainable which are:

- Legal Help – advice on rights and options and help with negotiating
- Help at Court – someone speaks on a person's behalf at court, but does not formally represent them
- Family Mediation – helps people to come to an agreement in a family dispute after a relationship has broken down without going to court. It can help to resolve problems involving children, money and the family home
- Family Help – help or representation in family disputes like drawing up a legal agreement
- Legal Representation – representation at court by a solicitor or barrister
- Controlled Legal Representation – representation at mental health tribunal proceedings or before the First-tier Tribunal in asylum or immigration cases.

Who can provide legal aid services

Legal aid services can be provided only by organisations which have a contract with the Legal Aid Agency (LAA) as mentioned above. These include solicitors in private practice, law centres and some Citizens Advice Bureaux. A person can only get civil legal aid for the following types of cases:

- Welfare Benefits
- appeals to the Upper Tribunal, Court of Appeal or Supreme Court.
- Council tax reduction schemes
- appeals to the High Court, Court of Appeal or Supreme Court.

123

- Debt
- court action by a mortgage lender because of mortgage arrears.
- court action by a creditor to force a person to sell their home
- a creditor is making a person bankrupt.
- Housing
- court action to evict a person from their home because of rent arrears
- eviction from a home
- a person is homeless and needs help from the council with being re-housed
- a rented home is in serious disrepair
- a person is being harassed and needs a court order to protect them
- a landlord or the council is taking a person to court to get an anti-social behaviour order or anti-social behaviour injunction against them.

Discrimination

a person is being discriminated against and this is against the law. The law protects people from being discriminated against by employers, education, housing and service providers, public bodies such as the Council and associations like sports clubs.

Education (Special Educational Needs)

Appeals against Special Educational Needs assessments by the council

Immigration and asylum

- asylum applications

- a person has been detained
- a person is applying to settle in the UK (known as indefinite leave to remain) because their relationship has broken down because of domestic violence
- a person is an EC citizen and is applying to stay in the UK because their relationship has broken down because of domestic violence
- a person is applying to stay in the UK because they are a victim of trafficking
- proceedings before the Special Immigration Appeals Commission
- a person has received a Terrorism Prevention and Investigation Measure notice
- applications for asylum support, but only if a person has applied for housing and financial support.

Family, children and domestic abuse

People can get legal aid:

- for private family law matters, for example, divorce, dissolution of civil partnership, property, finance and children matters where there is evidence of domestic violence or abuse or child abuse. Domestic violence or abuse covers psychological, physical, sexual, financial or emotional abuse.
- if person is a victim of domestic violence or are at risk of being a victim of abuse, need advice on their rights to stay in their home and needs a court order to protect them.
- if a person is a victim of domestic violence or are at risk of being a victim of abuse and need advice on family matters such as divorce, financial disputes or disputes about children

- if a person needs to protect a child who is at risk of abuse - for example, they need to apply to court to prevent someone who has abused a child from having contact with them
- for family mediation
- for family court proceedings if a child
- if a person needs protection from being forced into marriage or because they have been forced into marriage
- if the local authority is taking court proceedings to take a child into care
- to stop children being removed from the UK or to get them returned if they have been unlawfully removed
- to enforce European Union and international agreements about children and maintenance.

Mental Health

- advice if someone has been detained or 'sectioned'
- applications to Mental Health Tribunals

Court of Protection work

- appeals against DOLS (Deprivation of Liberty Safeguards).

Community Care

- for community care cases. Community care services are arranged by the council for people with care needs such as home help.

There is also legal aid for:

- a court order to protect a person from harassment

- an appeal against a decision stopping a person from working with children and vulnerable adults
- advice and help on Disabled Facilities Grants
- civil claims relating to allegations of abuse and sexual assault
- confiscation proceedings
- an injunction for gang-related violence
- an inquest into the death of a member of a family
- an injunction to stop a nuisance caused by environmental pollution
- cross-border disputes.

Legal aid is not available for:

- consumer and other contractual disputes
- most immigration cases

Criminal Injuries Compensation Authority cases

- private family law, for example, divorce, dissolution of civil partnership, property, finance and children matters, other than cases where there is evidence of domestic violence or abuse or child abuse. Domestic violence or abuse covers psychological, physical, sexual, financial or emotional abuse
- personal injury or death
- tort and other general claims
- conveyancing
- advice on will-making
- matters of trust law
- company or partnership law
- business law
- legal advice in relation to a change of name
- defamation or malicious falsehood.

Financial conditions for getting civil legal aid

Income and capital must be within certain limits to get civil legal aid. If a person or their partner receive a passporting benefit, their income will not be looked at to see if they qualify for legal aid. However, capital will be looked at. The passporting benefits are:

- Income Support
- income-related Employment and Support Allowance
- income-based Jobseeker's Allowance
- guarantee credit part of Pension Credit
- Universal Credit.

A person will get legal aid for an asylum problem if they receive government asylum support.

Legal aid if a person has income or capital

If gross monthly income is over £2,657 legal aid is not available. 'Gross income' means before tax and national insurance are taken off and it excludes certain social security benefits. If a person has more than four children, this limit goes up by £222 for the fifth and each additional child. A partner's income is included unless the partner is the person who they are in dispute with.

If gross monthly income is £2,657 or less, a solicitor or adviser will then check what disposable income is. To qualify for legal aid, disposable monthly income can't be more than £733. (2015-2016). If a person has disposable capital (savings) of over £8,000, they won't get legal aid. Disposable capital includes:
- money in the bank
- valuable items

- the value of a home (if owned). This depends on how much the property is worth and how much a mortgage is.

A partner's capital is included unless the partner is the person who the person is in dispute with.

If a person is getting Legal Representation and their disposable capital is under £3,000, they won't have to pay a contribution towards the costs of their case.

If a person has more than £3,000 of disposable capital, they will have to pay a contribution towards the costs of their case. This contribution has to be paid straight away and it will be all of the capital they have over £3,000 up to the total cost of the legal advice.

If a person owns a home, it will be considered as capital. However, not all the value of the home will be taken into account. You can deduct the mortgage or any charges on their home, up to a maximum of £100,000. They can also deduct 3% of the market value of the home (the amount for which it could be sold for on the open market) for sales costs. If a person is over 60, some of their capital can be disregarded in addition to any mortgage disregard.

Repaying a solicitor's costs at the end of the case

If a person has had legal aid and the result of their case is that they kept or gained money or property, they will probably have to pay back some or all of the costs of the case. This is called the statutory charge.

Civil Legal Advice helpline

If a person is eligible for civil legal aid, they may be able to get help from the Civil Legal Advice helpline. The Civil Legal Advice helpline gives free, independent and confidential advice on the following matters:

- debt
- housing
- family
- welfare benefits
- discrimination
- education.

Legal services for deaf people

The Royal Association for Deaf people (RAD) provides Information, Advice and Guidance (IAG) services to Deaf people in sign language on topics such as:

- benefits
- housing
- employment
- debt
- family.

Legal aid for criminal cases

Legal aid in criminal cases is organised by the Legal Aid Agency. There are different types of help obtainable, depending on circumstances.

Free legal advice at the police station

If a person is at the police station, they have the right to free independent legal advice from a duty solicitor. This does not depend on financial circumstances. Their request will be passed to the Defence Solicitor Call Centre. Alternatively they can choose their own solicitor and won't have to pay for advice if they have a contract with the Legal Aid Agency. The Call Centre will contact their solicitor for them.

If person is under arrest, they have the right to consult a solicitor at any time unless it is a serious case when this right can be postponed. They must be given an information sheet explaining how to get legal help.

Help before being charged with a criminal offence

A person could get help with a criminal case even if they haven't been charged with a criminal offence. For example, a solicitor could give general advice, write letters or get a barrister's opinion. This type of help is called Advice and Assistance.

A person will get Advice and Assistance if they get Income Support, income-related Employment and Support Allowance, income-based Jobseeker's Allowance, the guarantee credit part of Pension Credit or Universal Credit. If getting Working Tax Credit, they may get Advice and Assistance depending on income and personal circumstances.

Help with representation at court

There are three ways a person could be helped if they need to be represented in court for a criminal offence.

A Representation Order

A Representation Order covers representation by a solicitor and, if necessary, by a barrister in criminal cases. To qualify for a Representation Order in the magistrates' court, a person must meet certain financial conditions. They will automatically meet these conditions if they are under 18. Also they automatically meet the conditions if they are getting Income Support, income-related Employment and Support Allowance, income-based Jobseeker's Allowance, the guarantee credit part of Pension Credit or Universal Credit. Otherwise, the financial conditions depend on gross income and whether they have a partner and/or dependent children. If their gross annual income, which when adjusted to take into account any partner or children, is over £22,325, (2015-16) they will not be eligible for a Representation Order. However, in some cases it may be possible to apply for a review on the grounds of hardship.

If a person meets the financial conditions, they will usually get help with representation in a criminal case in the magistrates' court, as long as it's in the interests of justice that they are legally represented. For example, in the Crown Court, it will automatically be in the interests of justice that a person is legally represented.

Advocacy Assistance

Advocacy Assistance covers the costs of a solicitor preparing a case and initial representation in certain cases such as:

- prisoners facing disciplinary charges
- prisoners with a life sentence who are referred to the Parole Board
- warrants of further detention.

A person doesn't have to meet any financial conditions to qualify for Advocacy Assistance, except if it's a prison hearing.

Free advice and representation at the magistrates' court

If a person didn't get legal advice before their case comes up at the magistrates' court, they can get free legal advice and representation by the court duty solicitor. This does not apply to less serious cases such as minor driving offences but it could cover cases of non-payment of council tax. A person does not have to meet any financial conditions to get free advice and representation at the magistrates' court.

Paying court fees if getting legal aid

If a person wishes to start court action, they will need to pay a court fee. If a person is on a low income, they can get help with paying all or some of the court fee. This is called a fee remission.

If a person is receiving Legal Representation or Family Help (Higher) they cannot apply for a fee remission as their solicitor will pay their court or tribunal fee for them. If they receive advice under Family Help (Lower) where a consent order is being applied for, their solicitor will also pay their court or tribunal fees for them. A person can apply for a fee remission if they are receiving:

- Legal Help
- Help at Court
- Family Help (Lower) except where a consent order is being applied for.

Other sources of free or affordable legal help

If a person is not able to get legal aid, there may be other sources of free or affordable legal help, such as Law centres, Solicitors and fixed fee interviews (Some solicitors may give up to half an hour's legal advice for a pre-agreed or fixed fee. Some schemes may offer a certain amount of free advice. The fixed fee interview scheme does not depend on income or savings - the charge will be the same for everyone).

Conditional fee agreements

In all civil non-family cases a person may be able to enter into a conditional fee agreement with a solicitor. This means that if they lose the case, they will only have to pay the costs of the other side and, depending on the agreement, the expenses that the solicitor has to pay out, including any barrister's fees. If they win the case, they will pay there solicitor a higher fee.

Pro-bono (free) help

LawWorks

LawWorks may be able to arrange free legal help for people if they can't get legal aid or afford to pay for legal advice. It arranges legal help through free advice clinics, mediation and casework. www.lawworks.org.uk

Bar Pro Bono Unit

The Bar Pro Bono Unit provides people with free legal advice and representation in court and tribunal cases from volunteer barristers. It only helps people who cannot afford to pay and cannot get legal aid. A case must be referred to the Bar Pro Bono Unit by a solicitor or advice agency such as a CAB, law centre or MP. www.barprobono.org.uk.

****

Glossary of terms

Advocacy-Arguments usually addressed to a court

Attorney General-A law officer of the Crown who represents and advises the Government on legal issues. Is responsible for presenting report on the operation of the CPS to Parliament.

Bail-The process by which the court or the police decide whether a suspect/defendant should be released into the community until a trial date or further questioning.

Bench-Where more than one lay magistrate sit together to hear a case they are referred to as the bench.

Chief Crown Prosecutor-Member of the Crown prosecution Service who has the responsibility for the day-to-day operations of a Crown Prosecution area.

Clerk to the Justice-Responsible for the administration within the magistrate's court. Provides advice on legal procedures, such as sentencing issues, to magistrates.

Codes of Practice-Written documents created by the Home Secretary under the Police and Criminal Evidence Act 1984, which provide information and guidance for police regarding use of their powers.

Common law-Judge-made law, developed on a case-by-case basis. Also referred to as case law, developed through the doctrine of judicial precedent.

Conditional bail-form of bail with conditions attached, such as agreeing to keep away from certain places etc.

County court-First instance court that deals with low value, non-complex cases.

Cross-examination-The process by which a lawyer can question an opposing party's witnesses or even the defendant in order to enhance their clients case.

Crown court-Criminal first instance court, hears indictable offences/triable either way offences-jury determines guilt or innocence of the accused-judge administers sentence.

Crown Prosecution Service-The primary agency responsible for prosecuting individuals who have committed criminal offences within England and Wales. Also determines the charge that will be laid before individuals based on police evidence.

Custodial sentence-A form of sentence administered by the courts. Most severe form of punishment-defendant is detained, for instance, in prison to serve a sentence determined by the court.

Director of Public Prosecutions-Head of the Crown Prosecution Service. Can undertake criminal prosecutions in his or her own right.

District Judge (magistrates court)-Legally qualified magistrate who can sit and hear case on own-presides over cases in the magistrate's court.

Equity-A form of law based on principles of natural justice and fairness.

European Court of Human Rights-Court that hears infringements of the European Convention on Rights and Fundamental Freedoms.

European Court of Justice-Court of the European Union which is responsible for hearing actions between Member State, between Institutions and the Member States and between EU Institutions themselves. Also responsible for ensuring uniform interpretation and application of European Union law throughout the Member States.

Hearing-The oral submission in the litigation before the court, tribunal etc.

High Court-First instance civil court hears complex and high value cases. Three divisions: Family, Queens Bench and Chancery.

Hybrid offences-also known as triable either way offences. Offences of varying degrees of seriousness which may be heard by the crown.

Inadmissable evidence-Evidence which is not admitted into the trial proper. This may be that the evidence has been obtained in an improper manner.

Indictable offences-Most serious form of criminal offences, such as murder, rape, which can only be dealt with by the Crown Court.

Judicial precedent-The foundation of the development t of modern common law/case law. Process by which members of the judiciary follow previous case decisions where facts are similar.

Judicial review-A higher court's supervision of a tribunal's procedure.

Lay magistrate-A layperson, ordinary member of the public without legal experience who can sit within magistrate's courts determining guilt or innocence of defendants, sentencing issues, etc.
Layperson-A member of the public without legal experience who plays a role in the English legal system.

Legal Executives-Members of the Institute of Legal Executives who may have rights of audience in some courts.

Legal Services Commission-Government Agency responsible for administering legal aid, legal representation etc.

Magistrates court-First instance court which has primarily criminal jurisdiction but also some civil jurisdiction.

Majority verdict-Verdict where those in favour of a particular verdict outweigh those opposing.

Mitigating circumstances-Circumstances particular to a defendant, which are taken into account by the courts when determining sentence.

Obiter dicta-Latin phrase which literally means 'things said by the way'.

Original precedent-The first decision on a particular legal problem which is novel in nature.

Practice directions-Instructions issued by a court concerning the conduct of cases generally.

Pre-action protocols-Standard steps which each party should effect prior to issuing a claim or prior to a hearing.

Proceedings-Steps to start or pursue a case in court.

Ratio-decidendi Latin phrase, literally meaning, reason for the decision'. The binding element of a judgement.

Remand-Where a person has been refused bail, he or she will be held in custody until the trial takes place.

Representation-Appearing on behalf of a client.

Rights of audience-The right to appear as a lawyer in a particular court.

Royal assent-Monarch gives formal approval to a bill becoming an Act of Parliament.

Sentence-Pronouncement of the court, which highlights a form of punishment that is to be imposed on a defendant convicted of a criminal offence.

Summary offences-Minor criminal offences that can only be heard in the magistrates court.

Triable either way offences-Offences of varying degrees of seriousness which may be heard in the Crown Court or magistrates court.

Tribunal-A panel authorized to adjudicate on specific matters.

Ultra vires-Acting beyond powers given.

Youth Court-A special court within the magistrate's court which hears criminal cases involving young offenders.

****

Index

Acts of Parliament, 4, 19, 33
Administrative law, 3, 14
Admiralty court, 6, 77
Anti-social behaviour orders, 116
Anti-Terrorism, Crime and Security Act 2001, 87
Appeals in criminal cases, 107
Appellate Courts, 79
Arrest for breach of the peace, 92
Arrestable offences, 7, 90
Attendance centre orders, 9, 112
Attorney General, 6, 64, 65, 99, 102, 108, 119

Backbenchers, 35
Bail, 8, 97, 98, 99
Bail Act 1976, 97
Barristers, 5, 57, 58, 59, 60, 61
Binding precedent, 3, 24

Chancery Courts, 21
Children Act 1989, 78, 101
Christians, 17
Church of England, 33
Circuit judges, 5, 62, 63, 105
Citizens Advice Bureau, 95
Civil law, 14
Claimant, 16
Commercial court, 6, 77
Commission for Equality and Human Rights, 95
Commission of the EU, 43
Committal proceedings, 8, 103
Common law, 3, 20, 21
Community sentences, 9, 110
Community Support Officers, 95
Complaints against solicitors, 5, 58

Complaints against the police, 95
Constitutional law, 3, 14
Contract law, 71
Council of Ministers, 4, 43
Council of the European Union, 43
County Court, 15, 16, 27, 61, 62, 63, 80, 81, 117
Court of appeal, 26, 108
Court of Appeal (Civil Division), 6, 80, 81
Court of Appeal (Criminal Division, 26, 65, 107
Courts of first instance, 27
Crime and Disorder Act 1998, 113
Criminal Appeal Act 1995, 108
Criminal Defence Service, 10
Criminal Justice Act 2003, 86, 98, 101, 107, 109, 110
Criminal Justice Act of 2003, 39
Criminal Justice and Public Order Act 1994, 86, 87, 91, 94, 98
Criminal law, 3, 14
Criminal Procedure and Investigations Act 1996, 105
Crown Court, 8, 15, 16, 27, 62, 63, 65, 96, 97, 100, 102, 103, 104, 105, 106, 109, 116, 117, 118, 120
Crown Prosecution Service, 8, 16, 57, 58, 60, 64, 65, 96, 99
Curia Regis, 20
Custodial sentences, 8, 110
Customs, 3, 19

Defending a claim, 6, 73
Defining law, 3, 16
Discharges, 9, 111, 114
District judges, 5, 63, 64
Divisional courts, 26

Equitable remedies, 7, 83
Equity, 3, 21
Euro, 47
European Central Bank, 43, 46
European Constitution, 41, 42

European Court of Justice, 3, 4, 25, 26, 43, 44, 45, 46, 48, 49, 81, 108
European Economic Community, 41
European law, 5, 25, 39, 41, 45, 49, 81, 108
European legislation, 19, 34
European Union Amendment Act 2008, 42
Exemplary damages, 7, 82

Family division, 78
Fines, 9, 101, 111, 113
Fingerprints, 94

General Council of the Bar, 57, 59
General customs, 3, 19
General damages, 7, 82
Green paper, 34

High Court, 4, 5, 6, 15, 16, 26, 27, 58, 62, 63, 72, 73, 75, 77, 78, 79, 80,
   81, 105, 117
High Court Judges, 63
House of Commons, 33, 36, 38, 64
House of Lords, 4, 8, 25, 26, 33, 35, 36, 37, 38, 79, 108

Inferior courts, 27
Inferior judges, 5, 62
Injunctions, 83
International law, 3, 13

Judicial precedents, 3, 22
Judiciary, 61
Juries, 9, 117, 118, 119, 120

Kings Chancellor, 21

Law centres, 10
Law Society, 57, 61
Legal aid, 9, 121

Legal Services Commission, 9
Lisbon Treaty, 42, 46
Literal approach, 51
Local customs, 3, 19
Lord Chancellor, 21, 60, 61, 77
Lord Justice of Appeal, 62
Lords Justices of Appeal, 5, 62, 63
Lords of Appeal in Ordinary Law (Law Lords), 26

Magistrates, 6, 8, 15, 16, 27, 58, 61, 63, 64, 79, 96, 97, 99, 100, 101,
    102, 103, 104, 109, 111, 112, 117
Magistrates Courts, 15, 63, 100, 101
Master of the Rolls, 62
Misuse of Drugs Act 1971, 87
Moral values, 17
Muslims, 17

National Assembly for Wales, 26
National law, 3, 13
Nominal damages, 7, 82

Obiter Dicta, 23
Original precedent, 3, 23

Parenting orders, 9, 115
Parliament, 4, 19, 33, 34, 35, 36, 37, 38, 39, 43, 51, 53, 55, 56, 64, 87,
    90, 109
Parliamentary Counsel to the Treasury, 34
Persuasive precedent, 3, 24
Police and Criminal Evidence Act (PACE) 1984, 86
Police interviews, 8, 93
Police powers, 7, 86
Powers of arrest, 7, 90
Powers to detain suspect, 8, 92
Powers to stop and search, 7, 87
Practice Statement, 4, 29, 31

Presumptions, 5, 55
Pre-trial hearings, 8, 96
Private law, 3, 14
Private Members Bills, 35
Prosecution of Offences Act 1985, 65, 99
Prosecutor, 16
Public law, 3, 13
Purposive approach, 5, 51

Queen's Counsel, 60
Queens speech, 34

Ratio Decidendi, 22
Recorders, 5, 62, 64, 105
Rectification, 84
Reparation orders, 9, 113
Reporting cases, 4, 32
Rescission, 7, 83
Right to silence, 8, 94
Rights of detained people, 8, 93
Roadside checks, 7, 88
Royal Assent Act 1961, 37
Search warrant, 89
Sentencing, 8, 109
Serious Crime and Police Act 2005, 85
Serious Organised Crime Agency (SOCA, 85
Sex Discrimination Act 1976, 48
Solicitor General, 64, 65, 102
Solicitors, 5, 57, 58, 61
Special damages, 7, 82
Specific performance, 7, 83
Summary offences, 96
Summary Trials, 101
Superior judges, 5, 62
Supervision orders, 9, 113
Supreme Court, 3, 6, 26, 27, 30, 31, 33, 45, 62, 80, 81, 104, 108, 117

The Court of First Instance, 4, 46
The ejusdem generis rule, 5, 53
The fast track, 74
The golden rule, 51, 52
The Independent Police Complaints Commission, 8, 95
The indictment, 105
The literal rule, 5, 51, 52
The mischief rule, 5, 52
The multi-track, 74
The small claims track, 74
Treaty of Rome, 41, 44, 45, 47, 108
Triable either way offences, 96
Tribunal, 16, 44, 80

Unfair Terms in Consumer Contracts Regulations 1994, 47
Unlawful entry, 7, 89
Voluntary searches, 7, 87

White Paper, 34
William the Conqueror, 20
Woolf Report of 1999, 71

Young offenders, 9, 112
Youth Court, 101